Carving the
Native American

Carving the
Native American

Step-by-Step Techniques
for Carving & Finishing

JOHN BURKE

FOX CHAPEL
PUBLISHING

© 1991, 2014 by John Burke and Fox Chapel Publishing Company, Inc., East Petersburg, PA.

All rights reserved. *Carving the Native American* is a reprint of the 1991 version originally published by Countrytime Press under the title *Carving the American Indian, Volume I* in the United States of America. This version published by Fox Chapel Publishing Company, Inc., East Petersburg, PA.

ISBN 978-1-56523-787-2

Library of Congress Cataloging-in-Publication Data

Burke, John, 1940-2010.
  [Carving the American Indian]
  Carving the Native American : step-by-step techniques for carving and finishing / John Burke.
    pages cm
  Includes index.
  Summary: "Carving the Native American takes the reader step-by-step through the creation of an expressive Native American bust. From starting with a clay model, to blocking out your carving, to shaping and detailing the tiniest curves of the face, all the way to staining and finishing, it guides you through the entire process of sculpting a large lifelike bust. Both beginning and veteran carvers will discover practical techniques and strategies to apply to any large sculptural carving. Sketch guides are provided to help you shape a realistic face, along with comprehensive instructions and hundreds of revealing photographs of work in progress. The author's original sketches and personal sidebars throughout this book offer revealing insights for a new generation of sculptors. A beautiful full color gallery presents an inspirational selection of his most magnificent work"-- Provided by publisher.
  "Carving the Native American is a reprint of the 1991 version originally published by Countrytime Press under the title Carving the American Indian, Volume I in the United States of America."
  ISBN 978-1-56523-787-2 (pbk.)
  1. Wood-carving. 2. Busts. 3. Indians in art. I. Title.
  TT199.7.B862 2013
  736'.4--dc23
                          2013001437

To learn more about the other great books from Fox Chapel Publishing, or to find a retailer near you, call toll-free 800-457-9112 or visit us at *www.FoxChapelPublishing.com*.

Note to Authors: We are always looking for talented authors to write new books. Please send a brief letter describing your idea to Acquisition Editor, 1970 Broad Street, East Petersburg, PA 17520.

Printed in China
First printing

Publisher's Note

The dedication and love of woodcarving that John Burke felt throughout his life shows in this updated edition of his book *Carving the American Indian*. It is visible in the extensive detail of the step-by-step instructions, in the friendly tone of John's writing, and in the several brief personal essays he includes throughout the book that, while not involving carving directly, truly reveal his personality and love of life. Though John lost his battle with cancer, his peers, pupils, friends, and readers remember him for the talented carver and gracious teacher he was.

When John was in his thirties, a friend handed him a knife and wood and encouraged him to give woodcarving a try. John started carving and never looked back, continuing to carve for the rest of his life. John's skills and personal carving style evolved greatly after he started carving with mallets and chisels, the larger tools allowing him to explore larger carvings. As John gained expertise over the years, people started asking him to share his techniques, and so for more than 20 years before his death, John taught carving classes in a variety of locations around the country. In fact, John pioneered many of the methods used to teach woodcarving today, and his techniques have influenced many of today's top carvers.

Author and carving instructor Jeff Phares (*Carving the Human Face*, Fox Chapel Publishing) attributed his carving career to John. "If it wasn't for John, I wouldn't be where I am today," Jeff said. "A lot of carvers wouldn't be doing what they are doing now without John. I consider him family. John hired me as an assistant teacher for three years and gave me my own class in 1991. I've been teaching ever since."

A popular figure in the woodcarving community, John was one of the earlier carvers to start up figure and bust carving classes in regions of the United States and Canada. Known as a generous man and a patient teacher, in his classes John concentrated on teaching projects that centered on frontier life, like Native Americans, mountain men, and gunfighters. John was especially known for his highly detailed, realistic busts. John also created the Burke Sharpening System, which is one of the most popular power-sharpening systems available today.

According to Desiree Hajny, the 2003 *Woodcarving Illustrated* Woodcarver of the Year and an emeritus member of the Caricature Carvers of America, John and his wife, Nancy, worked hard for many years to promote the art of woodcarving. "John introduced me to various tools and helped me learn to maintain my tools," Desiree said. "I absorbed as much knowledge as I could from him and Nancy."

Nancy continues to build the Burke Tool Sharpener and work with carvers today. "John was one of those rare artists who never confused profusion of detail with skill or talent. Carvers regarded him as a force of nature," Nancy said. "John always said that your work should say what you want it to say, not what others want to hear. His sculptures told genuine stories, told them without John having to say a word."

John's dedication to the art of woodcarving shows not only in his teaching legacy, but also in his writing. In addition to *Carving the Native American*, John is the author of *Carving America's Legends* and *Buffalo Dreamers*.

I visited John's workshop in rural Nebraska many years ago. It was the type of place where you could easily lose yourself for a few hours. Non-carvers may have found it a bit odd or even scary; all around there were reference boxes of animal skulls and bones, air-driven impact wrenches sporting big sharp chisels, and twisted stumps and other funky found wood. But John was greatly respected by fellow carvers who shared his appreciation for such things. They valued him highly as a member of the woodcarving community.

I hope that readers enjoy learning to carve the impressive Native American bust featured in this volume, and that John's works continue to inspire new readers for many years to come.

Alan

—Alan Giagnocavo

Acknowledgments

Getting this book ready for the printers was not an easy task. I knew before I started that I would need input and encouragement from many sources. When I sat down and started counting these people, the list was overwhelming. So my sincere apologies to those I missed or forgot to write down. Your names may not be on these pages, but they are in my heart.

Nancy, my wife and pillar of my life, without whom I would be unable to perform the smallest of tasks.

Kim, Kris, and Kerri, my three daughters. It is through their heritage that I stay close to the subjects I carve.

Annie, thanks to you dearest, for the opportunity you gave me to succeed. Without you, I'd still be welding tractors and this book would never have taken seed.

Barbie, thanks. You've been more than just a friend.

The ideas and advice I've gotten from you have been the start of some of my better works. Your opinions, tempered with the caustic sauce of reality have helped my work improve while keeping my head from swelling too big.

And to my father, who taught me the value of hard work and commitment. It took me a long time to realize what he was saying, and I still don't always do his words justice, but they have helped when I needed them...

And to all of the other artists, teachers, students, and hangers-on who have influenced me, both good and bad.

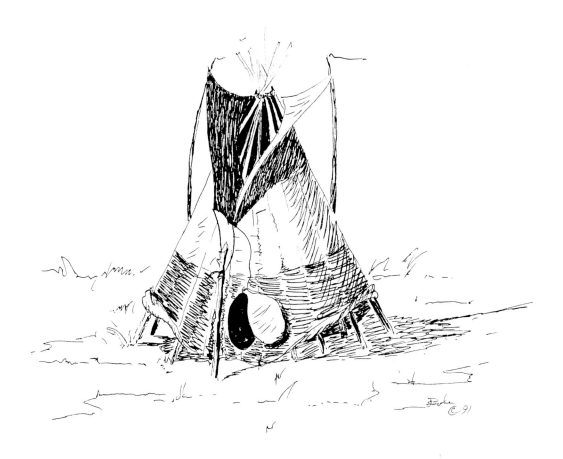

Contents

Gallery of Author Art

John Burke was a prolific and talented carver who excelled at his specialty in carving Native American busts. He utilized many types of wood to create unique, expressive faces. Featured in this gallery is just a small sampling of his work, both of Native American figures and a variety of other busts. Use them as inspiration for your own carving projects.

Mohegan, carved in 2009.
PHOTO BY MARC FEATHERLY.

The Listener, found wood carving.
PHOTO BY JACK A. AND CAROLE WILLIAMS.

Buffalo Hunter.

Blackfoot Medicine Man.

Magua, carved in 2009.
PHOTO BY MARC FEATHERLY.

Sven.

Red Wing.
PHOTO BY MARC FEATHERLY.

Mississippi Blues, carved in 2008.

Yellow Smoke.
PHOTO BY MARC FEATHERLY.

Cedar Chief.
PHOTO BY MARC FEATHERLY.

Hunts the Running Wolf.

Cedar Chief.
PHOTO BY MARC FEATHERLY.

Pueblos.

Black Elk.

Bear Coat.

– Introduction –

The ideas for this book first took form several years ago when friends and former students began suggesting that I compile my ideas and techniques into a volume suitable for use in the studio.

Although I had been toying with the idea myself for some time, I did not yet feel ready for the attempt. There were some things in my own mind I felt were not sufficiently developed yet.

Well, three years later, I realize that the questions are never completely answered. Each step in our development as an artist is merely a key that unlocks the door to a room full of deeper mysteries and secrets. One can only strive to do the best he is capable of at any one time in his life.

Progress in the development of one's artistic prowess, unfortunately, is not a gradual ascent, but rather a series of levels or steps, with each preceding level taking longer and becoming more difficult to obtain. It is at these later stages of development that many individuals falter, as they lack the discipline to sustain them as they assimilate more knowledge and ideas from others into a viable resource that can be physically impressed upon a suitable medium with enough vigor and emotion to make a visual impression on others. Such knowledge comes from studying and interpreting the work of others. We, as individuals, can progress only so far on our own. All of the great masters of the past studied under others. They admired and learned from their contemporaries.

This is much the way it came to me—a little at a time.

I sought out and took classes with people, who in my opinion, were tops in their field. From this slowly evolved a style of carving that showed what I was trying to say. This, too, I hope should be your goal. Not to mimic or duplicate what someone you admire has done, but rather incorporate segments of their work into something that is uniquely yours.

It is my sincere wish that what I show you on the following pages will help you in some way attain that goal.

CHAPTER 1

Getting Started

Before we go any further, I had better tell you this is not a book showing or telling you what to do, but rather I am going to show you how I start and finish a carving.

Now understand that not everything I talk about and demonstrate here is necessarily going to be the whole truth according to popular well-known textbooks. It is, however, structure and composition as I see it.

There are three things you are going to need to do the larger sculptural carvings we are demonstrating in this book:

Some suitable tools.

Some sort of carving screw to hold the wood down.

Some sort of heavy bench to bolt the carving down.

Then I suppose you also need some wood, so I guess that would make four things you need. Let's talk about some of these things for a few minutes.

Tools: contrary to some beliefs, you don't need a lot of tools to successfully execute a large, sculptural project. But, there are some tools you cannot do without. You would be amazed at the number of people who show up for a class with a sack full of homemade chisels that look like they were beat out of rakes, hoes, and files; for all their good intentions, this is just not going to cut the mustard. The following is a list of tools you can't do without.

- #3 or #4—¾" (or 18mm)
- #3 or #4—½" (or 12mm)
- #6—¾" (or 18mm)
- #6—½" (or 12mm)
- #11—½" (or 12mm)
- #11—⁵⁄₁₆" (8mm)
- V-tool—⁵⁄₁₆"–½" (8–12mm)

Optional tools that would be nice to have: these you can add later one at a time as you see fit.

- #3—1" or 1⅛" (25 or 30mm)
- #3—2" (or 50mm)
- #5—2" (or 50mm)
- #7—2" (or 50mm)
- #9—1⅛" (or 30mm)
- #11—¾" (18–20mm)

Understand that this list is not the law, so to speak, and that other tools can be substituted for some if they are somewhat similar in size and shape.

I am assuming that you already have a general assortment of small hand tools that are used for small whittling projects. You will also need a good knife with a long pointed blade. I rarely use a V-tool except for developing some structure, as I prefer a "soft" approach when I do the detailing of my carvings.

Shape Up and Sharpen Up

This is as good a time as any to bring out the subject of sharpening your tools. I have but one thing to say and that is if you can't suitably sharpen all of your tools, then you will never be an accomplished wood carver. Why anyone would not want to face this fact and learn, instead of imposing on others to do it for you, is beyond me. There is no comparison to the "high" you get when you can walk up to a sharpener and say, "Move over turkey. Let me show you how it's done."

My wife, Nancy, has been selling our own sharpening system, the Burke Tool Sharpener, for years. The hundreds she has made and sold are testimony to their effectiveness. If anyone would like information on the machines that she builds, contact Western Woodcarvers, 868 Co. Rd. 13, Ithaca, NE 68033; 402-623-4292; *www.westernwoodcarvers.com*.

The Carving Screw

This, simply put, is a device having a suitably aggressive thread on one end such as a wood screw. After drilling a pilot hole, it will thread itself into the wood. The other end should have a machine thread that will accept a wing nut so the entire thing can be tightened down on a bench, carving arm, or other suitable holding device. I'll show some pictures of these things on one of the following pages.

The Carving Bench

This can be almost any workbench, stand, or holding device that is heavy enough to withstand some heavy-duty hammering. These flimsy little workmate bench affairs, I am afraid, would prove very unsatisfactory. You sure as heck aren't going to hold it in your lap. I guarantee you will lose body parts along with receiving a lot of nasty cuts.

One other thing I'd like to mention, and that is I find it easier to stand while I carve. I can move around the piece more freely and have an overall better view of the entire work in progress. Sometimes I do sit when I am detailing some large areas or if I've had a rough one the night before.

Wood: The Raw Material

It goes to say that the grass looks greener on the other side of the fence. We are never satisfied with what we have close at hand. Somebody else or some other place always has just what we need to carve those wonderful divine inspirations. All I can say is there is merit in everything. An artist should be able to create wonderful things from almost anything. I do, however, have my preferences, and all of it is located on the other side of the fence.

I would be hard pressed to find a wood I enjoy carving more than Butternut, and I am fortunate enough to have a supply available in such quantity that I am able to reach as well as carve my own work in it. I have also used with success Red Cedar, Western Juniper, Black Walnut, and some Basswood. Each of these woods has its pros and cons. I think the project itself has a lot to do with dictating which or what is the suitable medium. Woodcarvers tend to be very resourceful and usually manage to find, trade or buy just about anything they want.

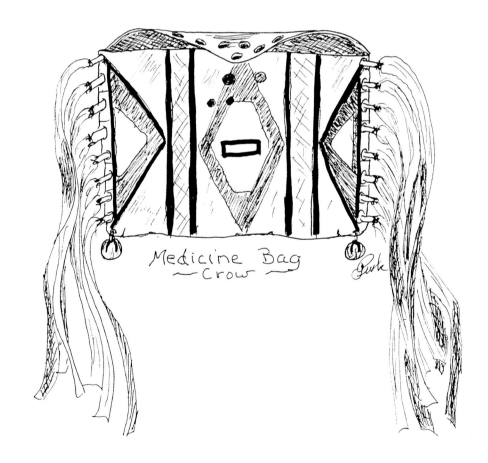

Medicine Bag
—Crow—

CHAPTER 2

Working with Clay

This shows how I get started developing a clay model. As you can see, I have made an armature with a base that can be lowered so that I can develop the clay from the top down.

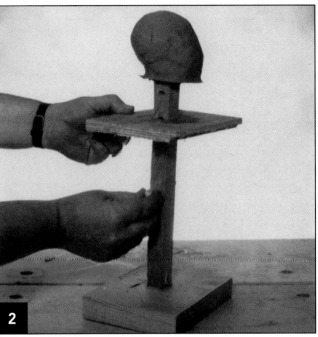

Here I have formed a mass of clay to represent the head and am lowering the base so that I may build up the upper body mass.

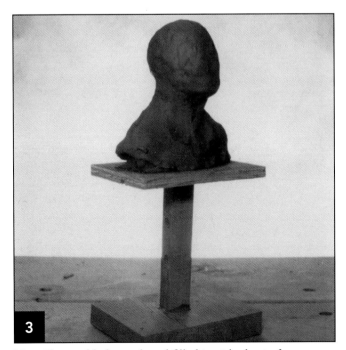

Now I have added a neck and filled it with clay to form a chest and shoulders. At this point I would probably wait for a day to let the clay dry enough to support itself on the stick when I lower the base.

After letting the model sit overnight, uncovered, I can now lower the base to a lower position to finish the model.

5

Here is the finished model. It really wasn't necessary to add so much detail, as all we really needed was the basic mass. But it is fun to practice sculpting different kinds of faces, so why not take advantage of the opportunity and get in a little practice before doing the wood piece. Chances are, before you finish playing around with the clay, you will come up with some new ideas for the finished work that you hadn't thought of earlier. You will probably discard some of those divine inspirations you had when you first started.

6

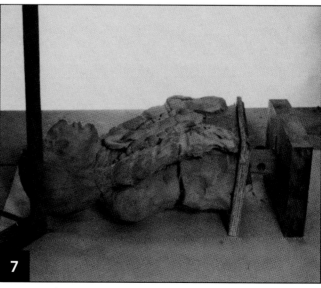

7

Now we're ready to trace the pattern onto a piece of stiff paper. I am using the tracing square to create a front and side profile. Note the importance of having the base of the armature square. Once finished and cut out, the pattern can be traced onto the wood you have selected and cut out on the band saw (steps 6 & 7).

— The Divine Inspiration —

Long before the white man and his glut of progress and civilization, a young man sought his vision, which was to be the major influence in the direction and extent of his goals in life. This vision was obtained only through great personal sacrifice and risk. Self-denial of basic subsistence in an area often fraught with danger where an enemy, man or beast, real or imagined, was of a constant concern—heck, roughing it to me is black and white TV.

Today we are a nation of excess. We drink too much, eat too much, drive too fast. We prioritize the casual relationship. What a waste, but I'm glad I did it.

We were heading south out of Santa Fe. It was early spring and although it was nice enough during the day, it would really frost your buns at night. I was riding with my old-time buddy, Mad Dog Martin, and we were heading for some tourist area called Ruidoso.

Since I pleaded innocent of any ability to drive safely, I found myself comfortably lodged in the passenger seat of the van. Old Mad Dog seemed to be alert and in good spirits. He alternately whistled and hummed some irritating Mexican song we had heard at a cantina the night before, Puta Del Oro, I think it was called. I, however, was suffering from a severe intestinal disorder brought on by an over consumption of bad water in the form of ice cubes.

We were hours south of Albuquerque when it happened. It took visual form as a small dark speck on the horizon which caught my eye as being just enough out of place to pique my interest. Straightening up from my sloughed position in the van seat, I became more erect as we drew near. Some inner thought warned my mind that the full brunt of this visual confrontation would be brief as we sped by, so I steeled myself and began studying the fast-approaching apparition in earnest. No amount of preparation could have prepared me for the full impact of what I saw as we sped past. Like a timeless transition from past to present, the young Apache stood, naked to the waist. He wore very baggy, tan colored pants of some thin, lightweight material gathered at the waist and held up with what appeared to be, in that brief moment, a large concho belt fashioned from Mexican coins. His hair was tied back with a traditional bandana and flowed, jet black, from withunder, to a near shoulder length where it again curled softly back under itself. In his left hand he carried a pair of old, rotting saddlebags filled with who knows what. In near shock, I knew I had experienced a divine inspiration.

I groped around and found a pencil in the glove compartment, and, on the back of a McDonald's sack, I hastily began sketching what I had just moments before witnessed. That night in the motel at Ruidoso, I further enhanced the sketch I had started. Our class with Lincoln Fox started the next day, so I immediately began sculpting my divine inspiration using some of the sketches I had done the previous day. Two days of intense frustration followed in which I produced nothing that even remotely resembled the magnificent Apache carrying a bag of who knows what in his hand. What sat before me resembled an Eskimo in a parka wearing snow goggles.

A painful lesson was accrued upon me that week, the results of which have initiated a fact of life that I practice and adhere to to this day. Don't use those divine inspirations until you have worked and played with them, added to them, taken some away, twisted and manipulated the thing until it begins to emerge as something that really approaches what you are trying to say. It will not look all that much like what you thought you wanted when you started. These great inspirations that seize us in our moments of lunacy should serve only as ideas to build upon in our search to create great sculptures.

CHAPTER 3

Cutting Out and Preparing the Wood

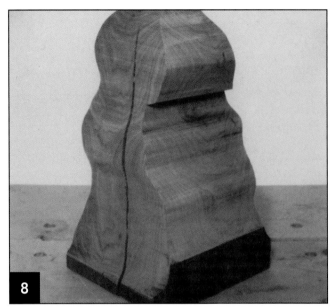

8

These next three views will give you an example in the progression of steps we are trying to achieve in blocking out and developing the basic structure of the carving.

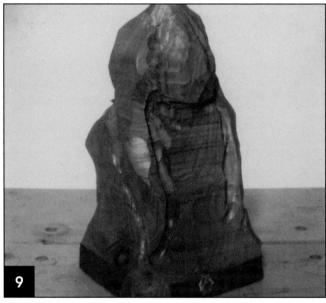

9

This is the sculpture after some of the corners have been rounded off and some of the hair mass has been separated from the chest.

10

Here the sculpture is fairly well blocked out and should give you an idea of what we are trying to accomplish in this first part of the book. Now let's back up and start at the beginning.

11

Here I am preparing the blank to accept a carving screw by drilling a suitable sized hole in the bottom of the wood. In this case, a ¼" drill bit was used.

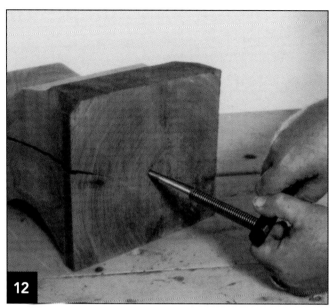

This shows me tightening one of the tapered carving screws Nancy makes into the bottom of the block of wood. The tapered threads on the one end of the screw are nice because if the wood comes loose, with a few turns of the built-in wrench in the handle, all of the threads are making contact with the wood again. An alternative screw can be made by welding a piece of threaded rod to a large lag screw and a piece of strap iron to a nut for a wing nut.

With the screw tightly in place, the work is now mounted on a holding device. In this case, I am using what is called a carving arm.

I am using a magic marker to determine the center of my face. This is important, since I am having the head turned slightly.

This shows me marking the hairlines for reference.

— Of White Mules and Men —

When my wife first transplanted this die-hard city boy into the country, I experienced something akin to a severe case of toxic shock. No 7–11's, no beer, pop, and other wasteful nonessentials of life I was accustomed to having close at hand. I mean, we were in the sticks. But I thought it might be a good idea to become assimilated into the local culture, so I set my hand to developing my green thumb and exhibit my prowess at growing things. I noticed my neighbor, Old Man Crosby, was copiously blessed with an abundant harvest of all manner of produce—ears of corn that looked like a "tow" missile, pumpkins the size of truck tires—the list was endless. So I proceeded to broach him on the subject of how in the heck he managed to do so good at gardening.

"John," he said, "Let me tell you how it is. If you want to grow good crops, you've got to till the soil with a white mule."

"But Crosby," I said, "How in the heck am I going to do that? You've got the only white mule in the county. You'll have to sell me that white mule."

"No way," he said. "I'd starve to death."

"Come on," I said. "Tell you what. I'll give you $500 for that mangy thing."

The offer was just too good for him to pass up. I paid him on the spot and then said, "Now Crosby, you're going to have to keep this thing until I get back from California next week."

"Done," he said. "I'll keep a close eye on that old thing."

When I returned to claim my prize, I announced, "Here I am Crosby. Cough up that mule."

He wouldn't meet my eye, and he said, "Darn, John, I can't do it. That sucker died last night. Choked on a carrot I gave him for a snack."

Only with great fortitude and strength did I maintain my calm and nonchalantly say, "That's okay, Crosby. I'll just take my money back then." But instead of my $500, he offered only the excuse that he didn't have my money anymore.

"John," he said, "I went downtown with that $500 with the intention of having only a beer or two. Well, you know how it is, one led to another, and, you know, everything looks good at closing time. I woke up and the girl and the beer and what was left of your $500 was gone, ppfftt, just like that."

Though it seemed that blows were imminent, I managed to say only, "Okay, Crosby, if that's the way it is, I still want the mule. You hook onto it with your tractor and drag it over to my place." The look in my eye held no questions for him. He knew he was about as close to dead as a man can get and still breathe. So he completed the task and made himself real scarce.

Well, a judicious amount of time passed and Crosby, obviously suffering a great amount of embarrassment, took great pains to avoid any confrontation whatsoever with me. But eventually a confrontation in the gas and shop did occur. Narrow aisles and fat butts don't make for a good opportunity to pass. Before I could even begin to speak, Crosby proffered these words. "John, I sure hope you ain't still mad at me. I'm really sorry about the mule and the money."

"Crosby," I said. "I'm not mad at you. Heck I made a lot of money off that mule."

"You're kidding," he said. "How could you possibly make money off that dead mule?"

"Easy, I had a raffle and sold 1500 tickets on that darn thing at $1 apiece."

"Really!" he stammered. "Didn't you have a lot of people mad at you when they found out?"

"Naw," I said, grinning. "Only the winner found out, and I gave him his dollar back."

CHAPTER 4

Rough Blocking the Carving

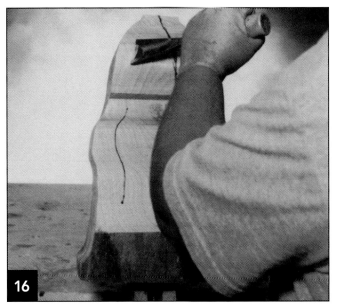

16

Now I start to round off the corners using a large 2" (50mm) gouge.

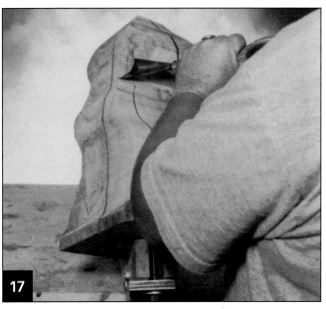

17

After three or four cuts.

18

This really gets to be hard work after a while, so I soon shift to using an air chisel. This is simply a cheap air hammer available from one of the many discount stores that proliferate around the country. Buy a cheap one. As I don't oil mine, when it wears out, I throw it away and get a new one.

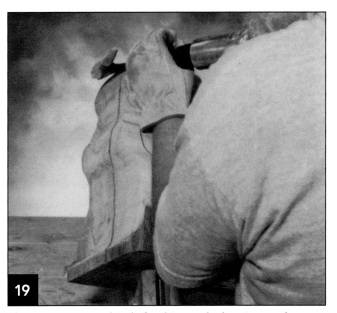

19

I hammer out my chisels for this gun by heating up the cutters that come with it and hammering them out to form a gouge of suitable shape and width. I then heat them up again and quench them to make the cutting edge hard enough to stay sharp.

 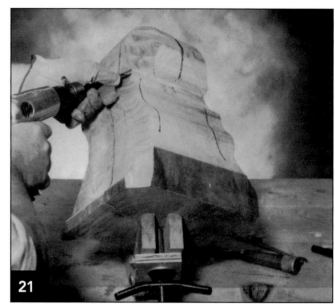

Rounding off the corners of what will become the hair (steps 20 & 21).

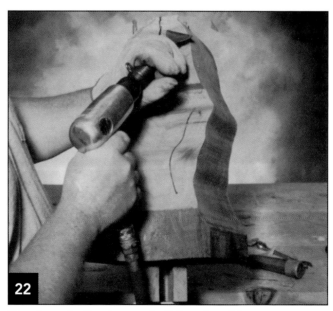

Here I am starting to round off the other side.

Rounding off more of the hair structure. Actually, most of this will end up being some sort of decorative wrap around the hair (steps 23 & 24).

Here I am making a stop cut along the underside of the chin.

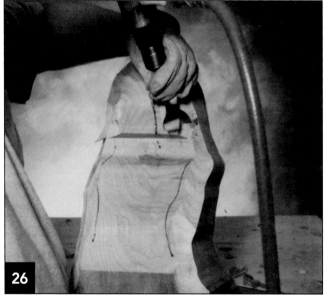

Now I am starting to shape the lower part of the face. It is important to remember at all times that the head is turned somewhat as we begin to develop the attitude or position of the head structure. This is really kind of tough the first few times you do it. All of our lives we have worked with right angles, parallel and perpendicular lines, all of the things we have been exposed and subjected to in our neat and tidy society. Now all of a sudden, you want to turn the head? Whoa, this is some pretty heavy stuff. Anyhow, turn it plenty because by the time we're through, it's going to work its way back a bit.

With the attitude of the face set, I am drawing the hairline in along the side of the face.

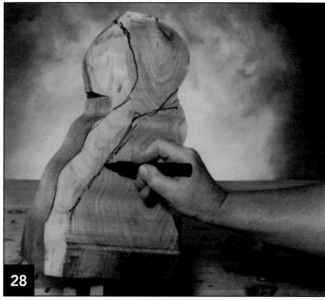

Now I am drawing the shape and size of the hair along the body. Remember! Keep the structure you are trying to create larger than what you think it will finish up.

Drawing the other side.

This technique of drawing the major areas on a carving is what I refer to as "visually separating the masses."

Here I am using a 1" (25mm) U-gouge to "physically separate" the hair away from the body.

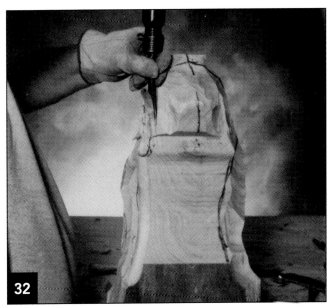

Separating the hair away from the neck.

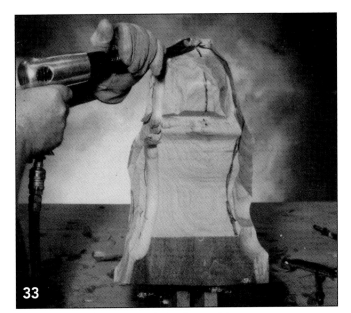

Now I am working around the face, taking care not to remove too much wood at this place. The reason I use a round U-gouge on all of these cuts is because this type of tool leaves a "wide" line, which on subsequent cuts, I can gradually "tighten" to the finished size.

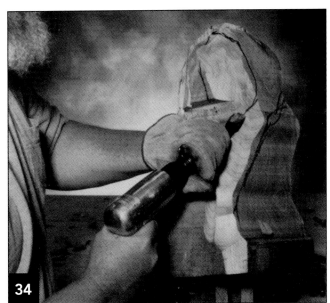

Here I am working on the other side.

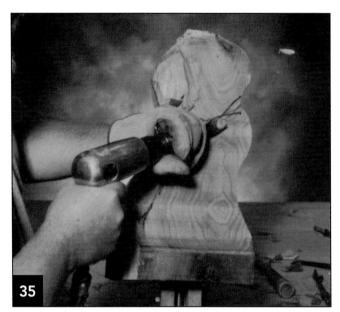

35

Now I am starting to outline, or separate the hair around the back of the head.

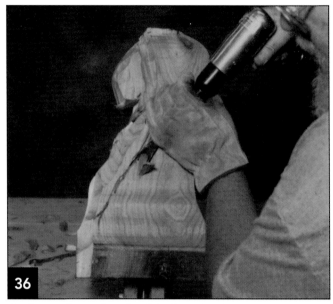

36

Outlining the underside of the hair that hangs down the front.

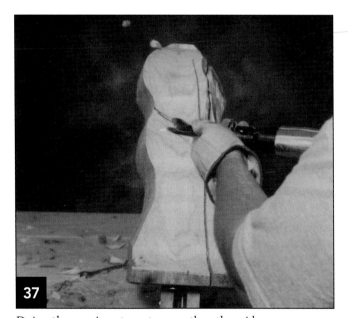

37

Doing the previous two steps on the other side.

38

Now I have switched to a large, medium-sweep gouge. About 2" (50mm) #5 sweep and am starting to round off the back of the head somewhat.

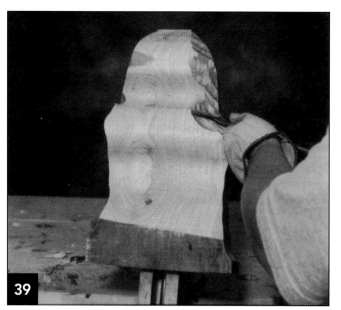

39

Using the same gouge, I am also rounding off the shoulder up to the hairline.

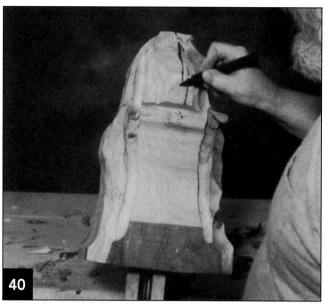

40

Here I am reestablishing the center line of the face as I prepare to round it off some more.

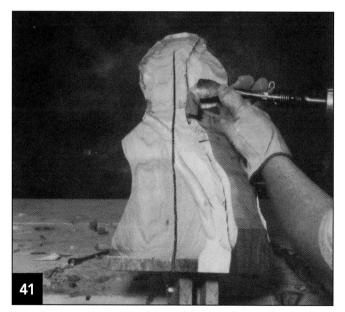

41

Now I am moving to the front of the carving, and I am beginning to round off the face a little more. Caution: at this point, make sure all of your cuts are toward the outside of the carving.

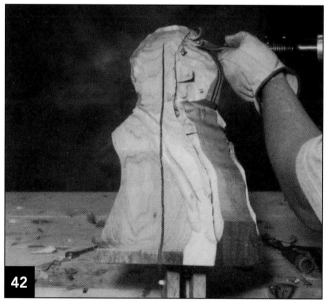

42

Here is another view as I continue to round off the face. Notice again how I continue to cut towards the outside edge.

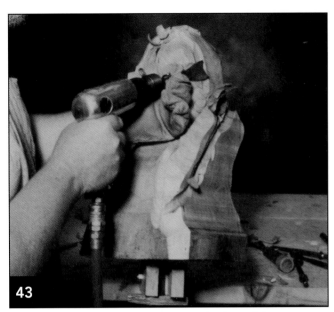

43

This shows me as I continue around the face of the carving.

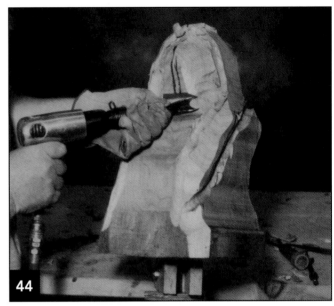

44

Now I switch back to a deep U-gouge and clean out some wood under the chin and along the jaw line.

45

I continue the same cuts along the other side.

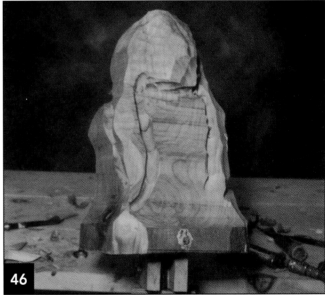

46

This shows the face nicely blocked out. No definite lines have been established yet and the structure has lots of material remaining for future development. Notice how far back the cut under the jaw line was extended into the hair. This is a good place to get really aggressive, as it helps carry the eye back into the carving. Notice, also, how I work at keeping the carving nice and clean. No rough looking cuts, fuzzies, or other crude situations on the wood. This is a very good practice to get into for all phases of the carving.

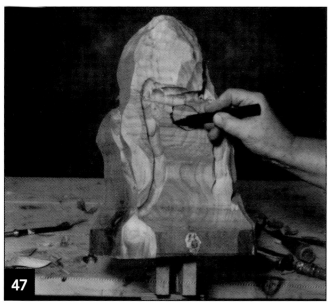

47

Now I am moving down into the chest area. I start by outlining the large shell gorget that will be hanging from the hair pipe necklace around his neck. Remember KEEP THE STRUCTURE BIG. By the time we are done whittling away at it, the finished size will be noticeably smaller.

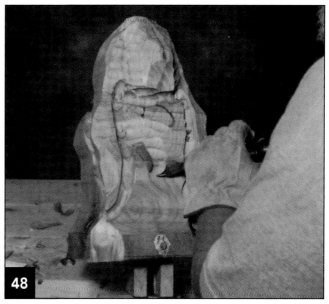

48

Now I am carving the chest back down below the hair. I try to form a slightly rounded structure, deeper where the chest and the hair meet. This really helps to isolate and strengthen the hair mass.

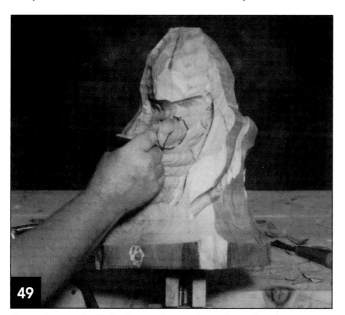

49

Since I carved off the lines when I shaped up the chest, I will reestablish where I want the shell gorget to go.

50

Using a medium sized U-gouge, I outline the gorget.

51

Here I am cutting around the top.

52

Cutting around the other side. Be sure to outline the leather ties hanging down from the center of it.

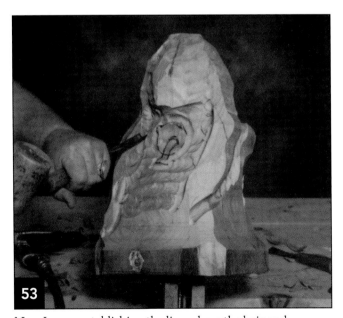

53

Now I am reestablishing the line where the hair and the chest meet.

54

I carry this cut right into that deep area along the neck that we developed earlier.

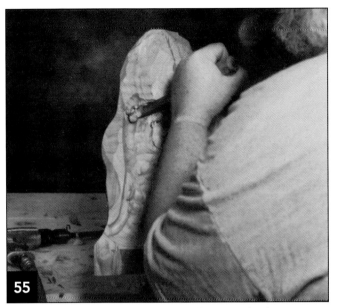

55

56

A cut from along the neck helps to clean out the fuzzies. This area, when finished, will create a strong shadow situated next to the face. This is the lightest or most reflective part of the carving and will create a strong visual impact.

Doing the same to the other side.

57

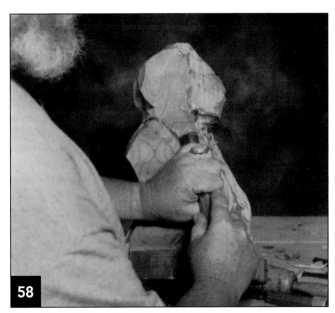

58

Using a large medium-sweep gouge, I begin to round off some of the hair.

Rounding off the underside of the hair.

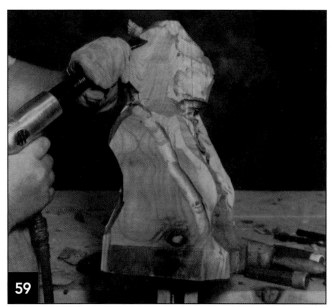

59

Back to the air chisel for some heavy-duty rounding off of the back of the head.

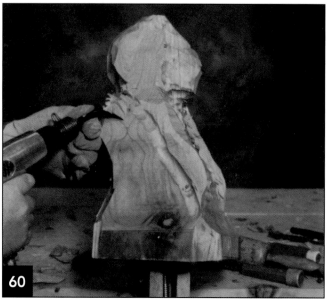

60

Here I carry the cut down to the shoulder area again.

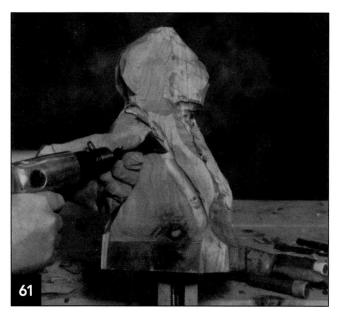

61

I carry this cut down along the chest until it disappears under the hair. All of these steps are repeated on the other side to develop whatever structure you may have there. One very important fact should arise from all that I have shown you so far. That is, we don't spend too much time on anyone part of the carving, but rather work on the entire sculpture at once, taking off a little at a time as we constantly work around the entire piece.

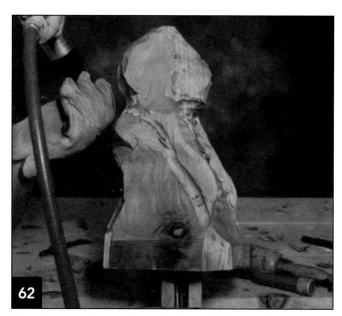

62

Here I am starting to shape the base of the carving.

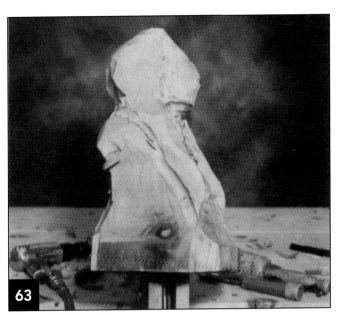

The base shape of the carving.

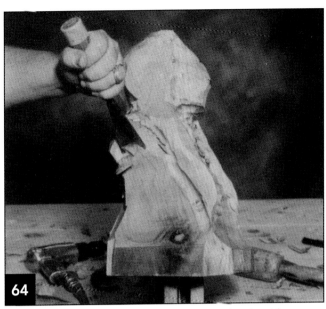

Using a 2" (50mm) #7 gouge to under cut the shoulders.

I carve down as far as I can to the apex of this depression, then cut across the grain to clean up the cut. It always surprises me how many people are not aware of this cleanup technique.

The cut going across the grain as previously shown.

CHAPTER 5

Making It Look Like a Native American

One of the really neat things about carving the human figure is the endless combination of different features that are possible. I would venture to say that no matter what kind of face you carve, within limits of reality, that somebody, somewhere, either does or has looked like it. It may have been one heck of a long time ago, but the possibility does exist. Even in the case of certain well-defined ethnic groups, almost any shape and profile can and does occur.

In the case of our subject, the Native American, one has only to look at some of the books of old photos and you will see individuals that look more like you and me than a proud Lakota Sioux. Years of careful, selective choosing and fanciful written descriptions, however, have undeniably created a somewhat stereotyped image in most people's minds. As such, most of us, myself included, have knuckled under to this pressure and prostituted our talent to some extent, to satisfy this idealistic image that exists in most people's minds.

I usually rely on two basic shapes to create my images, the most important being the side profile, and the second being the actual shape of the face when viewed from the front.

There are seven basic profiles that contain the elements for most faces. The following sketch will show you what I mean. I use #3 and #4 almost all of the time. Each one creates a completely different effect from young to old.

Seven Basic Profiles

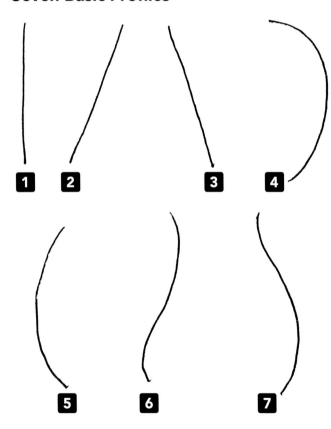

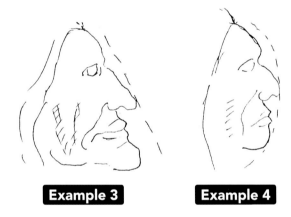

Example 3 **Example 4**

Above is a sketch of the seven basic profiles. Example 3 is the one I use to create old faces, while Example 4 is used to create a younger face. To the upper right is an idea of what I mean. For practice you should try drawing faces in the other profile sketches.

For the frontal view, I most generally use one of three shapes: square, round, or long. Below is a sketch to show you what I mean. There are some other ethnic features such as prominent cheek bones, noses, somewhat lower forehead, etc. Some of these things I'll bring up as we go along, some things I'll just flat forget to bring up. You know, sign #2 of old age, but I'm sure you'll manage to struggle through and I'll try to bring it up in another book.

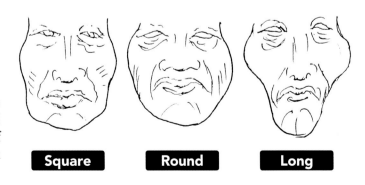

Square **Round** **Long**

Eye Detail

This set of drawings should help you understand some of the basic structure of the eye. Even though there are an infinite number of eye types we can carve, they all incorporate these same basic structures that I have just shown you.

With practice and study, you will soon be able to manipulate these structures to produce and convey any type of message and emotion you desire.

Eye sockets in the skull.

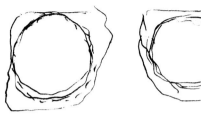

Eyeballs contained within.

Classic shape of the upper eyelids.

Classic shape of the lower eyelid at the opening.

Notice—the arrow indicates the widest part of the opening regardless of how wide or narrow you make the opening. This configuration must be maintained in some manner or another.

The iris, in a normal stage, is only about half visible and just touches the lower lid and disappears under the upper lid leaving about a half circle.

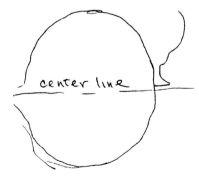

Sectional side view of the eyeball showing the placement of the upper eyelid.

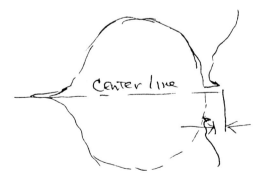

View of the lower eyelid in relationship to the upper—notice the lower eyelid is always behind the upper eyelid, no exceptions.

Basic Nose Structure

I imagine the nose is one of the most often messed up parts on a carved face. It's only because we don't take the time to understand it. When a problem becomes tough, we need to simplify it and break it down into parts.

The basic structure is something I would probably describe as a trapezoidal parallel piped pyramid, or in other words, a flat-topped pup tent.

It is within this structure that we can develop all of the components that make up a nose. Experience will teach you to allow ample structure for different size noses, but I do want to point out that the nose is probably the largest single object on most faces, with the exception of a few obnoxious "gum-beaters," and should be accorded enough material to enable one to develop its full prominence.

Study the drawings and the photos and then your own nose and see how some of these features play into your own face.

Remember, you are not going to get it overnight, but if you keep after it, you'll gradually become comfortable with the schnozze.

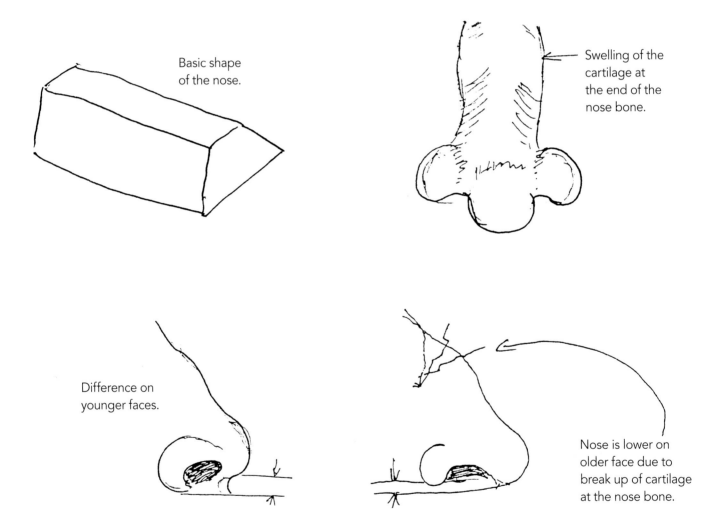

Basic shape of the nose.

Swelling of the cartilage at the end of the nose bone.

Difference on younger faces.

Nose is lower on older face due to break up of cartilage at the nose bone.

Mouth and Lip Structure

Here the problem, for the most part, lies in the fact that we don't make it large enough. The opening should be at least as wide as the center from eye to eye, but then you still have to develop the muscle structure that lies beyond that. So when developing the structure to the mouth, you actually end up with something about as wide as the outside corners of the eyes.

A strong, forceful approach will help you develop large structure. After carving a few basic mouths, you should try moving things around a bit. You know, raise one side, make him sneer, smirk, and smile or whatever.

Just remember, no matter how you move it around, you will still have the same muscle structure moving right along with you.

Again, I stress– study other people. Study these sketches along with the photos. Acquaint yourself with the various parts until you no longer have to keep looking in the book every time.

It's all a matter of interest. The more interested you are, the more you are going to do. The more mistakes you make, the more you learn.

Seven basic muscles of the lip structure.

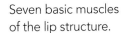

Two basic chin muscles.

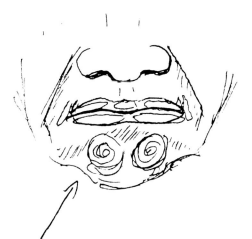

Most of the time, the chin muscles grow together—sometimes they separate—hence a cleft chin.

Upper lip usually has a slight flair. Lower goes under the upper before it reaches the corner of the mouth.

CHAPTER 6

Redefining the Sculpture

Now that we have the piece fairly well roughed out, we're going to move in close and start developing some of the individual masses.

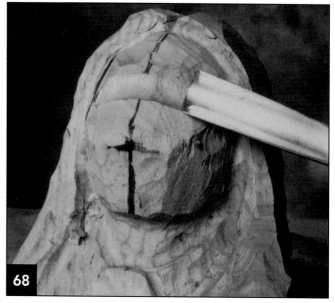

After drawing a vertical center line and a line for the center of the eyes and the end of the nose, I use a 1⅛" (30mm) #9 gouge to create a brow line, and at the same time, start to set the eyes back in.

This shows that initial cut. Always use the largest tools you possibly can. You'll have a much smoother carving in the end.

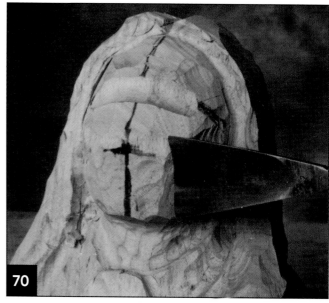

Here I am using a #7, 2" (50mm) gouge to create an area for the mouth.

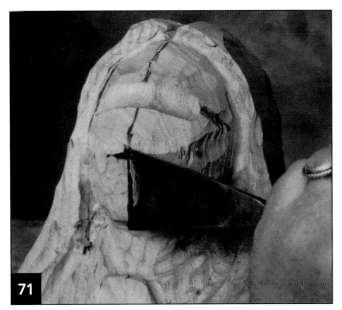

Notice that we also establish the approximate point that will become the end of the nose.

Carry this cut around and make sure both sides are pretty much the same.

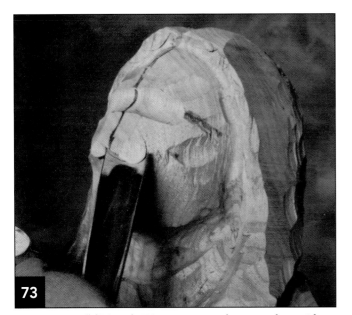

Now I use a 1" (25mm) #11 gouge to make a cut along side of the nose. Make sure to leave enough on each side of the center line to develop the detail later.

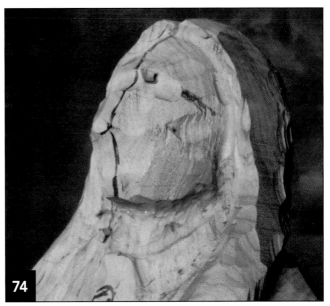

Extend this cut right on up to the previous one. This will start to form the inside corner of the eye.

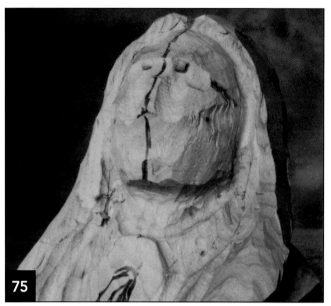

75

This shows both sides done. Notice how the remaining structure resembles a flat-topped pup tent. Well, it does to me anyway.

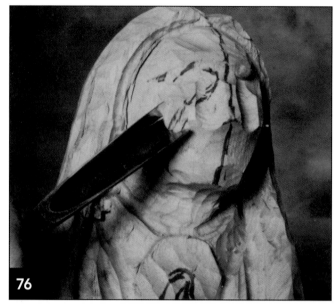

76

Study this photo and notice the "S" shaped line I have drawn on the side of the face. Using the same tool, this cut helps remove some excess wood from the cheek. Be aggressive. Different cuts result in different facial expressions; it's really hard to take off too much wood.

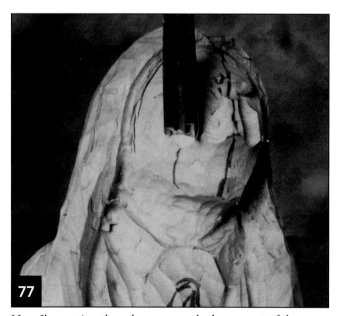

77

Here I'm cutting the other way on the lower part of the "S" line. This helps to set in where the corners of the mouth will end up. Remember, the radius of the dental curve is smaller than that of the face.

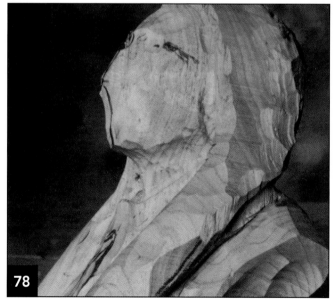

78

Here is a good view of the profile that I have established up to this point. Notice how massive the structure for the nose is. Small, dinky, incomplete noses are the ban of many woodcarvers.

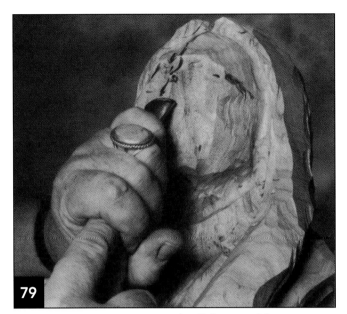

79

I am using a #5 gouge to smooth off the top of the nose. I carry this cut all of the way to the bridge, or brow line. This gives me plenty of length on the nose.

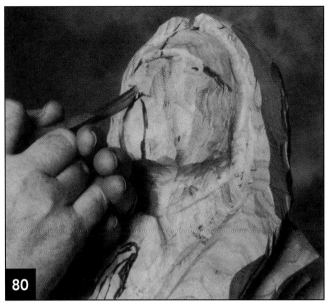

80

Now I am forming the sides of the nose. I want to leave a structure similar to a tent with a flat top. I'm still using a #5 or so gouge at this point. I think if you jump ahead a page or two you will see a better view of what I am trying to create. I really can't stress enough how important this initial blocking out stage is, so you must practice hard at observing people and other sources of reference so that you become familiar with the structure of the various parts of the face.

81

This gives a good idea of how the nose should look after it is blocked out. Remember, proper structure or foundation is the watchword here.

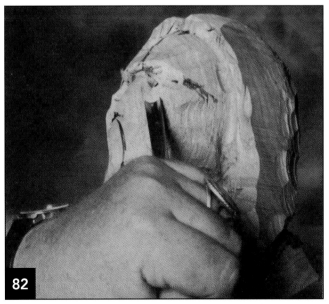

82

This is cut number one of the four cuts I use to block out the eye. Don't be afraid to go deep here, as this is about the deepest cut you will make on the face.

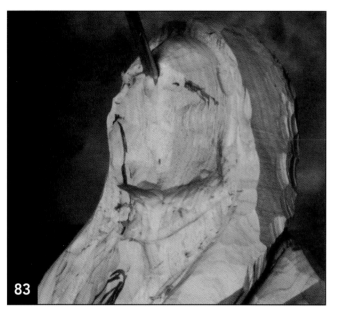

83

Here is cut number two. As you can see, I am cutting down from the top to meet the previous cut. I am using a #11, ⅜" (10mm) gouge on these cuts. If you are doing a smaller carving, then you would probably use a correspondingly smaller gouge. This is something that you learn by doing. Usually an assortment of about three or four sizes from ¼" to ½" (6 to 12mm) will get you through most projects.

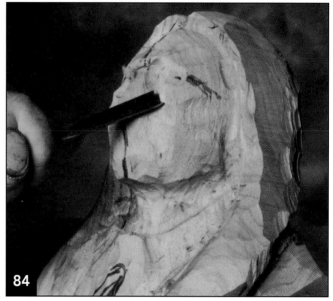

84

Cut number three. Here we start from the lower part of the eye again and cut upwards toward the outside corner of the structure. This point should be almost straight across from the front or inside corner of the eye. Here is a good place to use your mirror to help give you a better understanding of what I am saying.

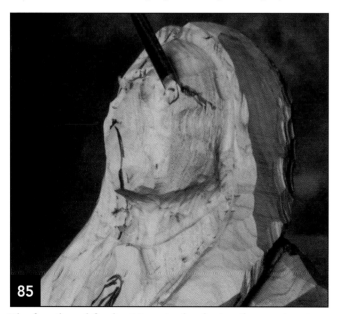

85

The fourth and final cut I use in developing the eye structure. Like before, I am cutting down to meet the previous cut in the corner of the eye. A little practice here and one can do this without leaving any fuzzies.

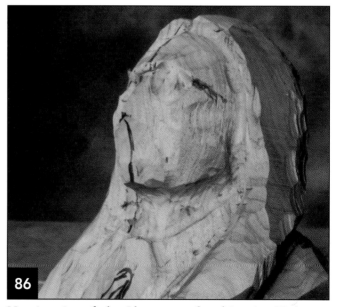

86

Here is a view of what I have created to this point. Notice again how large the initial form is.

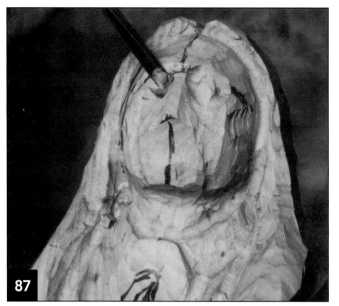

87

Here I am doing the same cuts as previously described on the opposite eye.

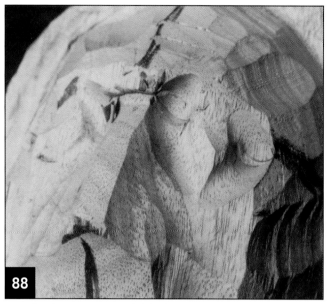

88

Here both eyes are rough-blocked out. At this point I usually play around with both sides until they are fairly well balanced.

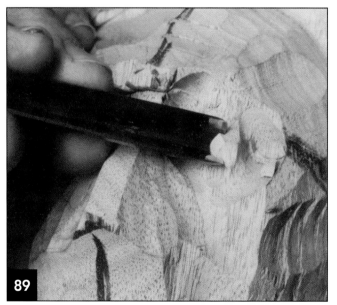

89

Now I use the same gouge or sometimes a shallower (#5) one to gently round off the knob I left with the previous cuts. I start my cuts from the center of the eye structure and cut to the outside of it.

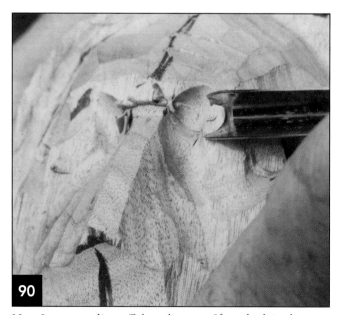

90

Here I am rounding off the other way. If you look in the mirror, you will see that I am trying to create a gentle mound upon which almost any amount of detail can be created.

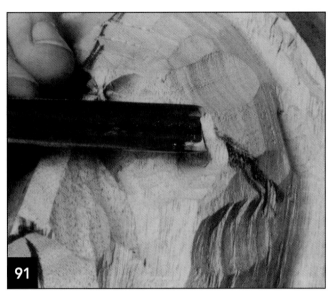

91

While I'm working in this area, I will remove some sharp edges from around the eye socket bone itself. Remember, everything goes from one structure to the other with that smooth transition of form.

92

Now I back up to the nose. Those of you with sharp eyes will probably notice by now that I am using several carvings of the same subject in this book. This is merely to speed up the process for the photographer, as I do a lot of preliminary work ahead of time on several pieces. Anyway, it shouldn't bother anyone who has a half of lick of sense. What I am drawing here is a reference line at the bottom of the nose, across where the nostrils would lie. This is to help keep me from carving the nostrils uphill and creating a nose with a large hook.

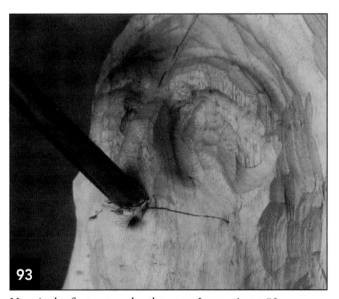

93

Here is the first cut under the nose. I am using a #6, ½" (12mm) gouge. I make this cut fairly deep.

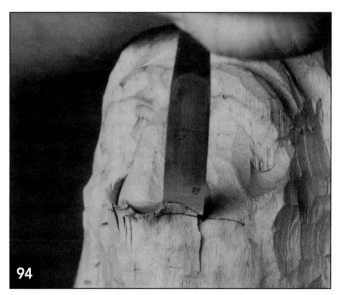

94

The same gouge used upside down to cut below the nostril. Notice how I am following the line I drew on the carving. Also, please notice I am cutting in perpendicular to the side of the nose. Read that again. Also, you will notice that all of these cuts are away from the nose structure. I do not do any straight-in cuts and especially no undercutting.

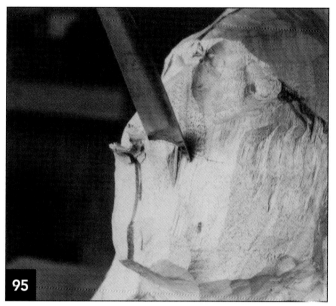

95

Here is another shot of the same cut from a different angle. Please, please, study these very important cuts.

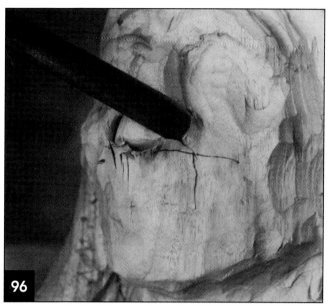

96

Here I am making cut number three. Using the same gouge, I slide down the side of the nose until it starts to cut, then force the gouge fairly deep into the wood.

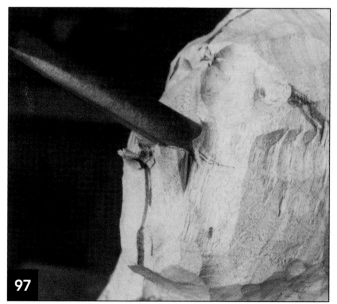

97

Same cut again from a little different angle. Remember, this is forming the outside of the nose, so be sure that you don't make this cut too close to the center and end up with a nose that is way too skinny. We can always pare it down if it ends up too wide.

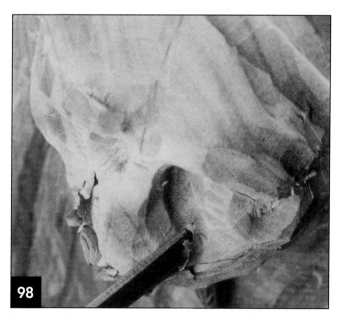

98

This view from above should give you an excellent idea of how this cut just slides down the side of the nose to where it starts to cut and form the outside edge and shape of the nostril.

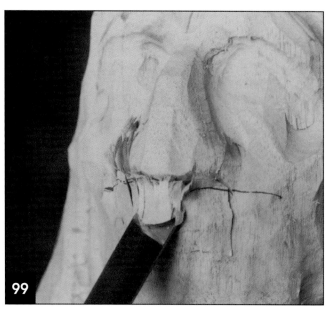

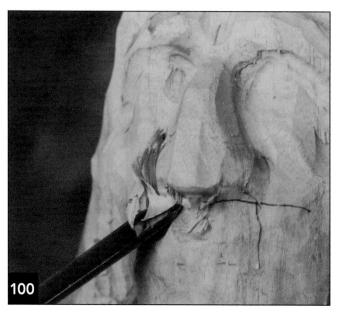

Using the same gouge, I start to clean up these cuts. Notice where I am starting this cut. I want to stay away from the area where the mouth will be.

The next cut cleans out under the nostril area.

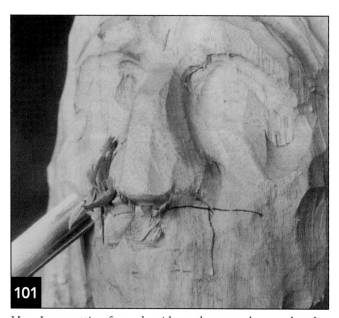

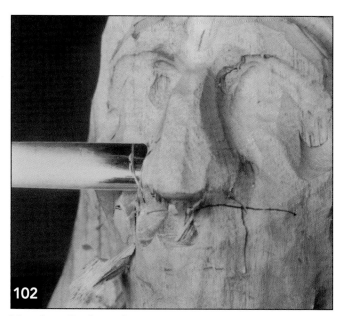

Here I am cutting from the side to clean out the wood at the outside edge of the nose.

Here I am finishing that same cut.

103

The same series of cuts on the other side. Notice again that I am not removing any wood where the mouth will lie.

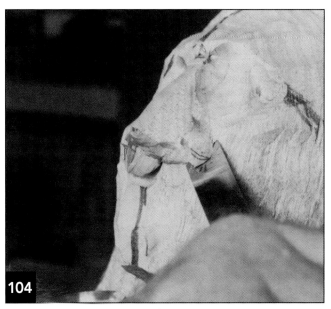

104

The cut at the outside edge of the nose again.

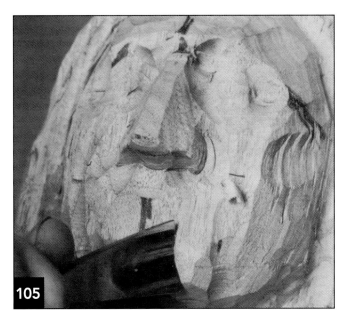

105

This shows the nostril area of the nose pretty well developed after this series of cuts. Also, I am starting to shape the chin down into the area that was relieved in the earlier stages of the blocking out process.

106

Now, here is great view of what I have established up to this point. Two large structures for the eyes, each containing a nice mellow mound of wood upon which we will later cut the detail for the openings. Also a large, strong structure for the nose that only needs a small amount of development later to finish it off, and a large expanse of wood below the nose which we are about to develop in the next series of photos.

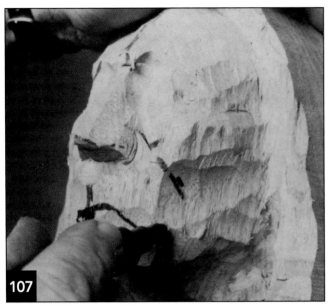

107

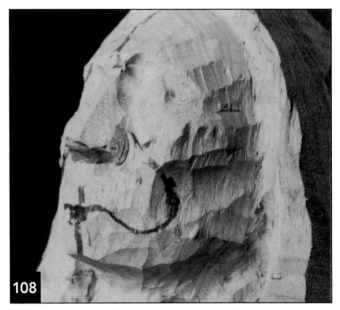

108

This shows me drawing a reference line around the muscle structure of the lips. This is only one of many versions possible, but regardless of what type of expression or emotion you are trying to create, it will always fall into this same general structure. We all possess the very same things as anyone else. They are only arranged a little different on each of us. Again, by studying the faces of many people, you will soon come to realize what I am trying to impress upon you.

This is the finished line. As you can see, it forms a variation of an "S" curve that we use so frequently throughout this carving.

109

110

Now I am starting the cuts necessary to isolate the structure of the mouth. Here I am making the first cut using a #4 gouge about ¾" (18mm) wide. I am holding it upside down so that the first cut is away from the nose. It's very important that you understand exactly where this first cut starts.

Here is the second cut. Notice how I am forming a gentle "S" curve again. Also, I am cutting straight in. I do not undercut at this particular point.

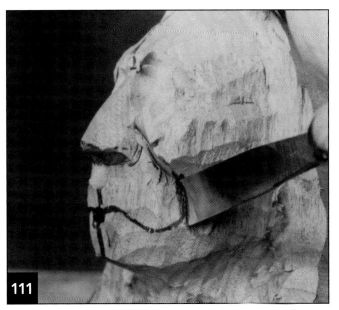

111

Here is the next cut. I have switched to a #6 gouge to form a little different shape. There is no set rule to these last few cuts. You just have to experiment and try different things on your own.

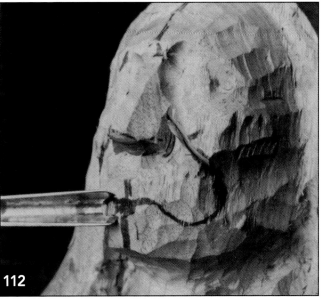

112

This cut actually separates the mouth from the chin. I am using a #11 gouge about ½" (12mm) on this cut.

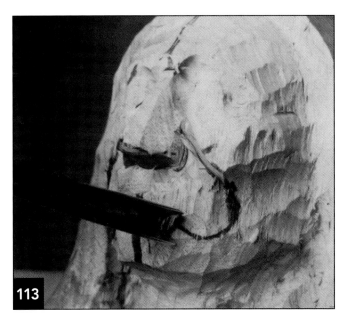

113

Here I am continuing the cut along the line. I will end up in the corner about where the previous cuts ended. The next several photos show this much better.

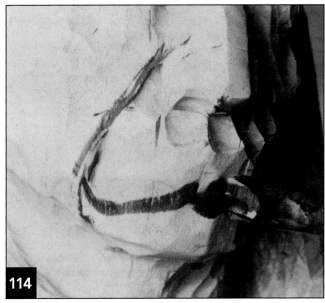

114

Here is the same series of cuts on the other side of the mouth. A good point to keep in mind here is that, although we are making similar cuts on each side, they should not be identical to each other. A little variation from side to side helps give the carving some "life."

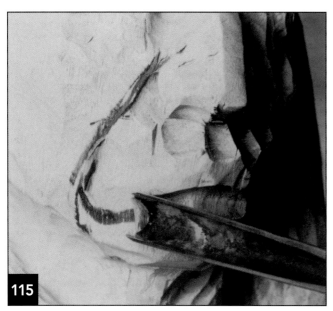

115

Notice how this cut is heading for the "corner" of the mouth.

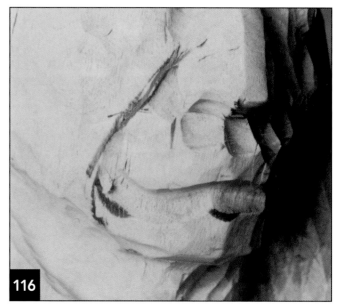

116

The finished cut. Now the mouth area is well defined and the chin has been separated from the rest of the face.

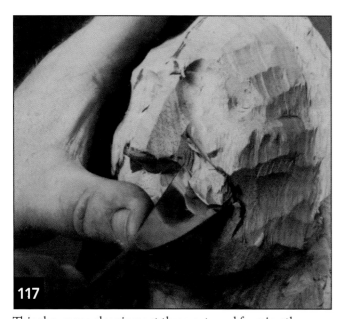

117

This shows me cleaning out these cuts and forming the "dental" curve.

118

Here I am shaping the lower part of the mouth. I am using a #6 gouge, but sometimes I might use a #4. I change tools and cuts all the time in an effort to find something new. You just have to keep experimenting until you find a style that is comfortable. And then you have to work hard at not "overusing" this style to where it becomes hopelessly stereotyped.

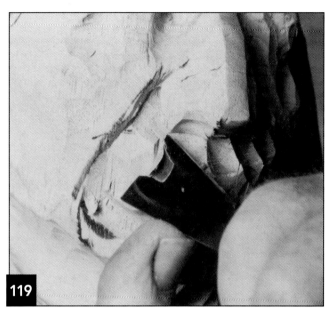

119

Now I'm cleaning up the other side of the mouth structure.

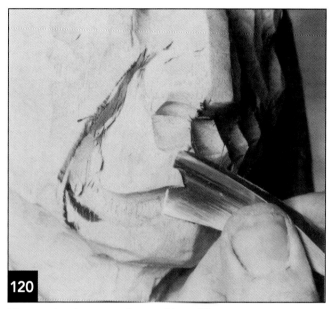

120

Here again, that smooth transition of form.

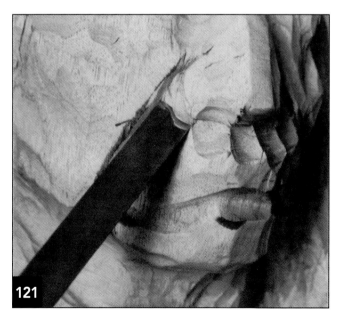

121

Cleaning up around the nose. Be careful that you do not undercut the nose. Again, I stress how important it is to keep your cuts nice and clean.

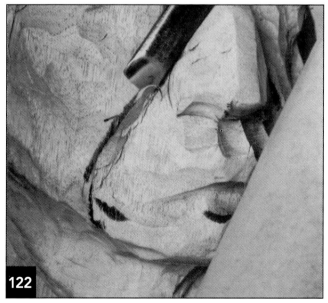

122

This shows my rounding off the sharp edge of this cut. You have to pay close attention to the grain, especially when working in butternut.

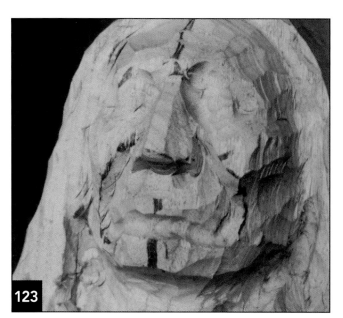

123

This is a great view of what I have accomplished up to this time.

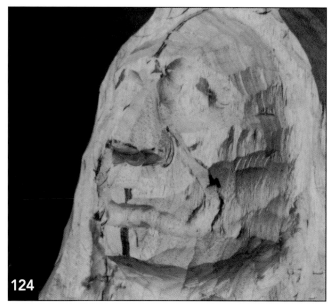

124

Another view from the side. Notice the nice round structure I created for the mouth. We should be able to go in later and detail out just about anything we want in the way of expression.

CHAPTER 7

Shaping the Front View

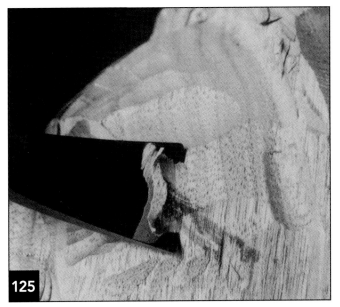

125

This next series of cuts is going to give us that strong, high-cheekboned look we like to see in sculptures depicting Native Americans. We are creating what I call a double "S" cut down each side of the face. I am using a #5 or #6 gouge on this first cut. What we are doing is narrowing the face at the temples.

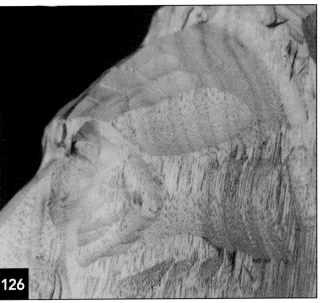

126

This is a view after the first cut. Try to keep all of your cuts heading out. Don't cut straight back in, and heaven forbid, don't undercut.

127

This shows me doing a little preliminary rounding off above the first cut. I carry these cuts clear back to the hair.

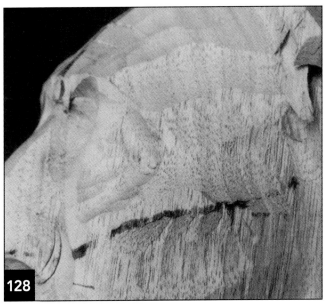

128

At this point, one should have a structure that looks something like this. If it doesn't, then maybe you should try carving animals or something…just kidding. Carry on.

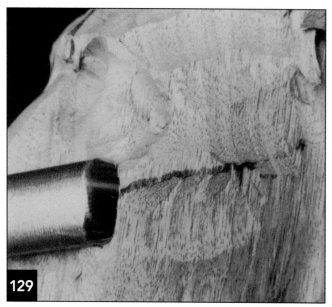

129

The dark line I have drawn here is the direction of the cheekbone, or zygomatic arch, if you prefer, as it lays on the face. Notice the slight angle. If I were to extend this line to the front of the face, it would intersect the nose at the tip. I am making this cut with the same gouge turned the other way around. Remember, cut to the outside and just scrape off enough wood to barely clean up the cut.

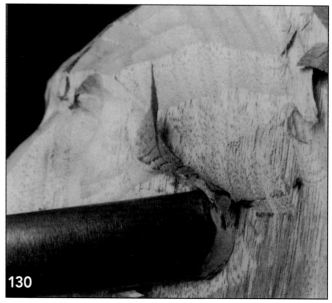

130

Here we are making the cut. Notice how little wood I actually remove.

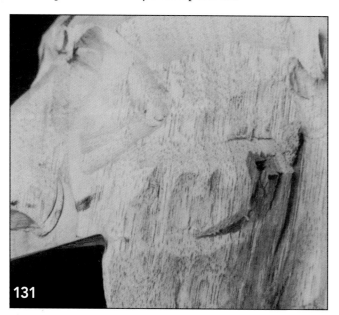

131

The previous cut being completed, I now reverse the gouge again and hollow out a bit of material underneath the cheekbone.

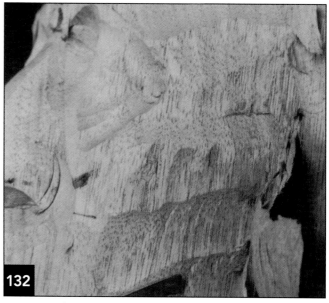

132

Here I am finishing up the lower part of the cheek. Notice again how I carry this cut clear back to the hairline. I don't always use the same gouges for this series of cuts. Oftentimes I use a combination of tools to produce different shapes of the face. This helps keep me from developing that situation where everything I do looks like the previous one.

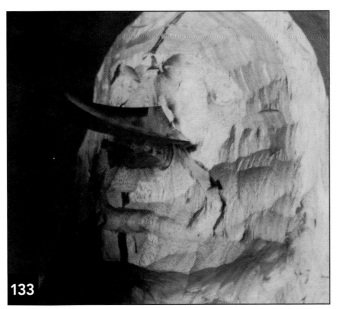

133

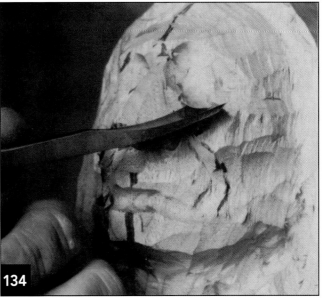

134

Now let's back up a little and develop the area above the cheekbone a little. Here I am using a #6 gouge to come off the nose with a nice smooth transition of form cut.

Then I come across the upper side of the cheek and cut slightly down into the eye socket.

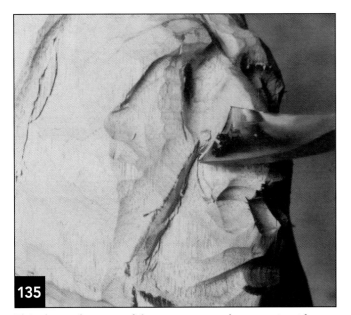

135

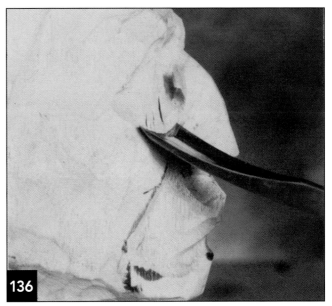

136

This shows the start of the same cut on the opposite side. Remember, use a smooth slicing motion across the top of the cheek when doing this cut.

Here you can see how I am "pushing" the structure of the eye further back into the face.

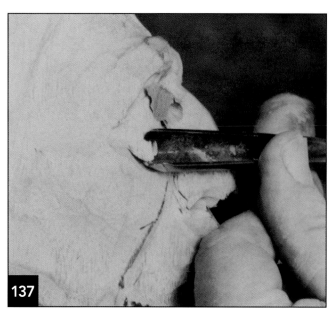

137

Now I am using a #11 gouge to clean up the previous cuts we just made.

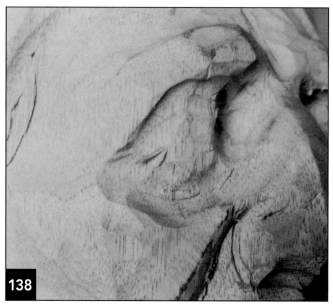

138

Here you can see exactly what I was trying to accomplish.

139

A good overall view of the carving up to this point. As you can see, both eye sockets appear to be fairly well balanced. The nose has a large imposing look about it. If you study the mouth area, you will probably see that it is a little lopsided, but not so much as to be out of place. This is good. What you see here is a good example of using distortion to create some really believable motion that will help to bring the finished carving to life.

140

A nice large U-gouge will make a "soft" separation of the brow line.

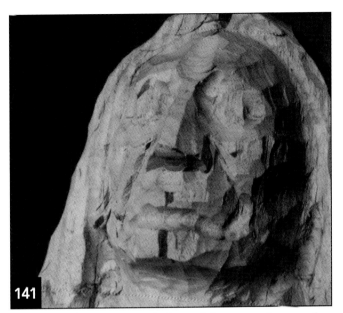

141

The finished separation. A little modeling around some of these sharp edges with a small shallow gouge will give a nice smooth transition of form to all of these components. While you're at it, remove a bit of wood from above the brow structure to make it a little more prominent.

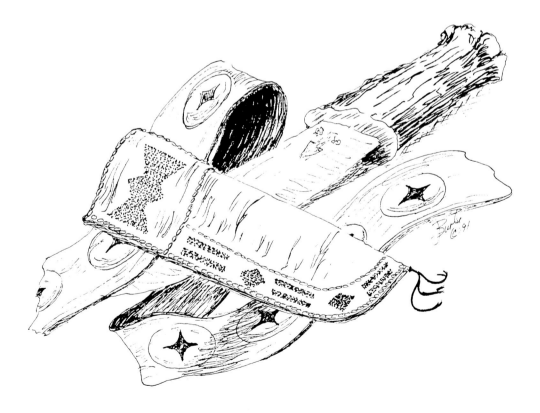

CHAPTER 8

Bringing It to Life

Without exception, every single drawing or anatomy book I have read brings up the subject of proportions and how they are laid out on the face. One eye, two eyes, four eyes, and on and on and on. This is supposed to be the "normal" situation that exists in most people. It's no wonder I see so much sculpture that looks like it is suffering from a severe case of rigor mortis.

You and I would be very hard pressed to find some poor schmuck who was afflicted with such a rare malady as to look like something in one of those textbooks.

Upon close examination of yourself, your wife, or someone else's wife, you will find that most of us have facial features that are somewhat softly distorted. You can't see it? The next set of sketches will give you some examples of what I am talking about and some successful compositions for using them.

Hopefully by now, I have stimulated your interest enough that you will begin to start looking for these situations to exist on other people and in photos.

This is really important, for it is by studying and learning to recognize these wonderful little nuances in the face, that we can learn to develop and utilize what will probably be our primary source of reference material.

These sketches show the difference between textbook drawings and real life.

In the first drawing, we have an example of what you see in many anatomy books. Everything is measured off to what any one individual might consider the "ideal" proportions of the face. Now please understand it is important that you have a strong understanding of these basic dimensions, for like every other part of the carving, we need a strong foundation to build upon.

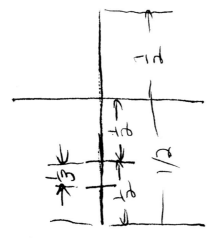

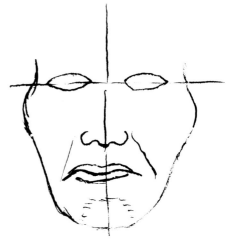

This set of drawings will give you an idea of what really happens in a person's face. The distortion can be used to various degrees of severity, one important thing to keep in mind is, as one line becomes distorted, all other lines tend to compensate in an artistically pleasing way. You will readily recognize this in the following drawings.

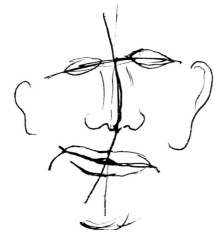

Very exaggerated but acceptable flow of exaggeration.

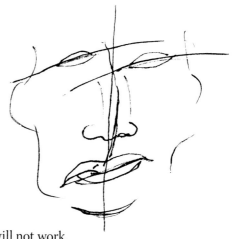

This will not work.

CHAPTER 9

Creating Detail

At this point, I have pretty well blocked out most of the major parts of this carving. There will be a few areas that will need to be brought up a little bit, but we can take those areas as we come to them. I have completed what is probably the most difficult part of the carving. You have to develop a tremendous amount of discipline so that you may successfully block out and develop the entire carving without succumbing to the temptation of carving detail too soon. Remember, "we will carve no line before its time." So all things said, let us now reward ourselves with the "fun" part of this project.

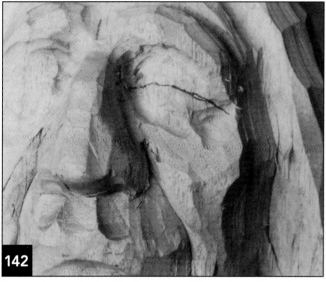

I am going to start with the eye on this project. Sometimes I start with the nose or the mouth. It really shouldn't make any difference as long as the structure is properly developed. What I have done here is to draw a reference line across what will be the center of the eye. Make thin, light lines so they don't become confusing later on.

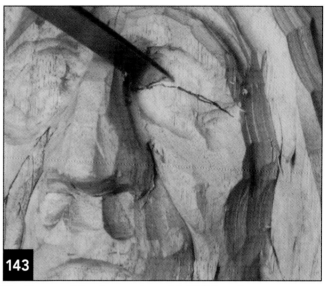

The first cut. Here I am using a #4, ⅜" (10mm) gouge to make the initial cut. I am cutting just above my reference line and forming the "bottom of the upper eyelid." Read that again…

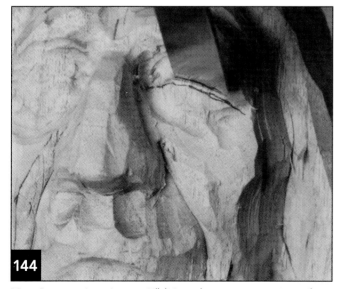

Here I am again using an ¾" (18mm) gouge to continue the cut towards the corner of the eye.

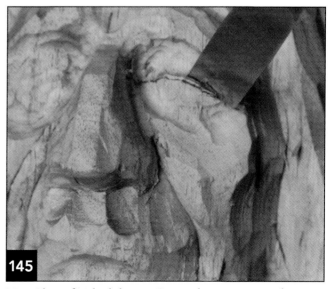

Here I have finished the cut. Remember to cut straight in. Do not undercut or cut in towards the inside part of the eye.

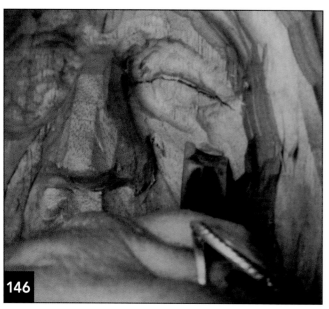

146

With this line established, I will now remove some material from underneath it. Notice how far down I am starting this cut.

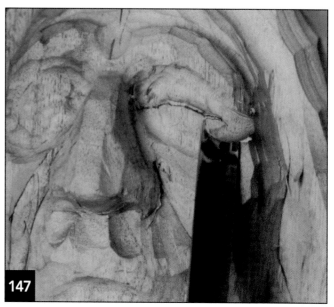

147

Carry this cut clear to the previous stop cut. I am using a #6, ½" (12mm) gouge in this case.

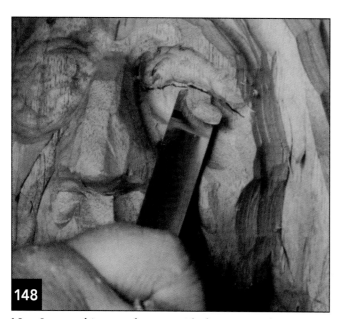

148

Now I am making another cut with the same tool.

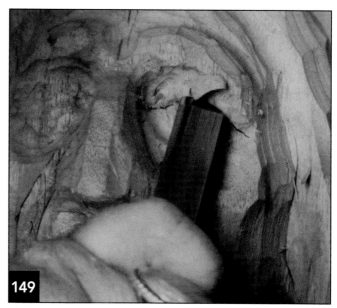

149

The most important thing to remember in this series of cuts is that you must maintain the contour of the eye that we so carefully developed earlier. We're keeping the same shape, just moving it back a little further.

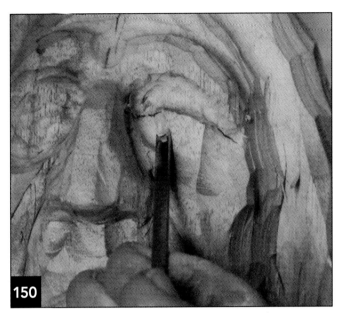

150

Here I switched to a smaller gouge to clean out the corner. You have to remember that this is only a general guide to what tools will work in any one case. Each sculpture requires its own individual approach. This you learn by doing it and doing it.

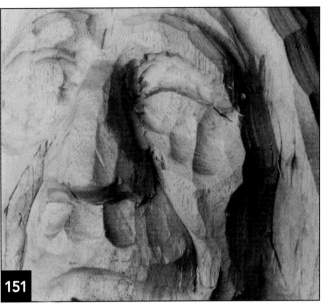

151

This shows the first series of cuts completed. Take a close look so you can see how I maintained the curve of the eyeball.

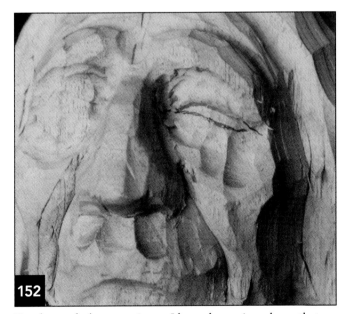

152

For the reader's convenience, I have drawn in a shape that can be used for the lower eyelid. This cut is probably a little bit stylized, but then, that's the way I carve. It's not good to get too tied down to one comfortable style. You're better off trying new things, even if they turn out as mistakes. Your carving will look looser and more natural for it.

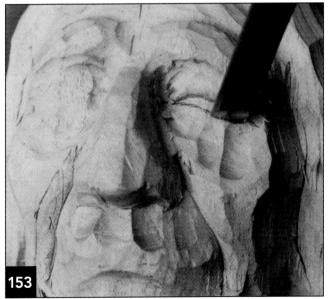

153

Now I am starting to cut the lower eyelid. This line will become the upper edge of the lower eyelid. Read that again. I use a gouge that best fits the shape of the line I am trying to create. When I feel really wild and brave, I will cut both of these lines freehand with a knife. You talk about getting a high off of something…

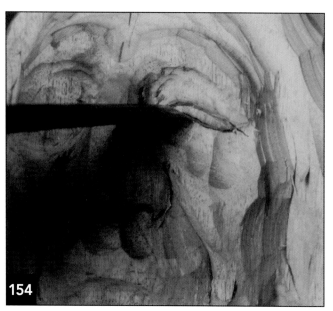

154

This gives you an idea of how I use a gouge to create this lower line. Remember a different shape of the gouge will give an entirely different shape to the opening of the eye, so keep trying different things and pay close attention to what sort of situations you create. After a while you will be able to match the style of eye you want to the carving.

155

The lower lid line completed.

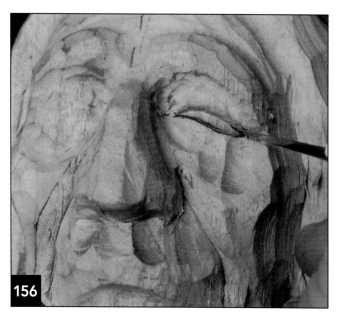

156

Now our labor is about to bear fruit. I shall begin to create the actual eyeball within all of this structure by first cutting a triangle-shaped wedge from each corner. This will start to create the roundness of the eyeball.

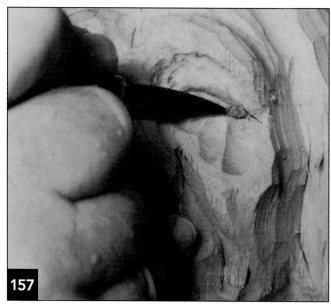

157

Here I am, using a sharp, pointed knife to cut out that little wedge shaped piece.

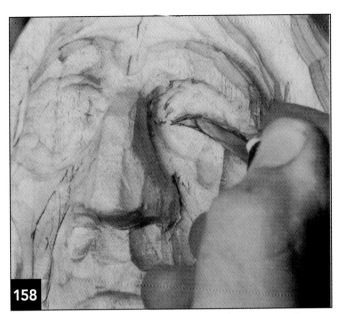

158

Here I am doing the same thing to the other corner of the eye.

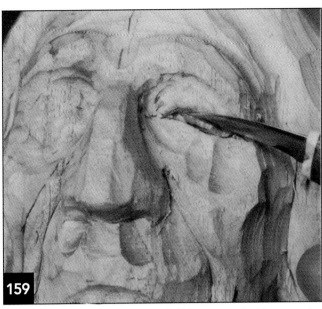

159

Now I shape the rest of the eyeball by using a knife to reach in and cut down and back so that I leave a nice rounded ball within the entire structure. Remember, it is important to cut down and back only when you are showing the actual eyeball. Otherwise, you will probably end up with eyeballs that look like footballs.

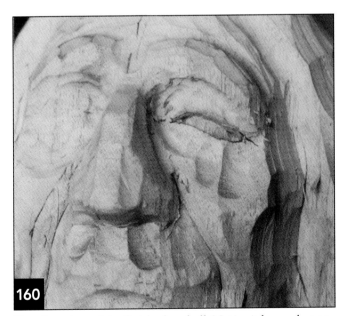

160

Here is a view of the finished eyeball. Notice it has only one plane to reflect any light. This is important.

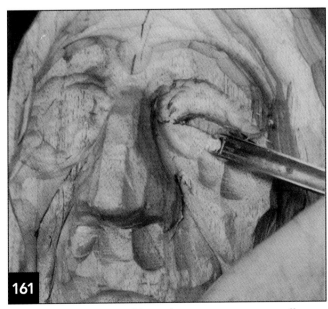

161

Now I am using #11, ⁵⁄₁₆" (8mm) gouge to create a small radius under the lower eyelid.

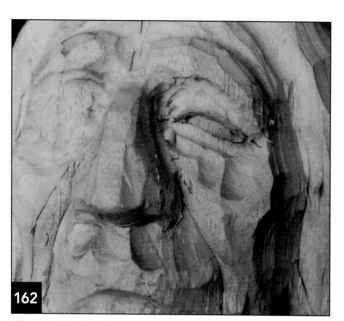

162

The completed radius cut under the eye.

163

The line I have drawn represents the amount of material I have to develop under the eye for that heavy "bag" full of wrinkles. This particular situation is different in every person. One should study people very closely to get ideas for different types of structure.

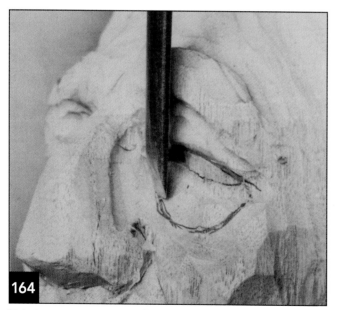

164

This is one way to create this heavy bag under the eye. I use a gouge that seems to fit the shape I want to create and make a cut around this area.

165

This shows my continuing the cut along the line. I don't really cut too terribly deep here. You could create the same similar shape by using a V-tool.

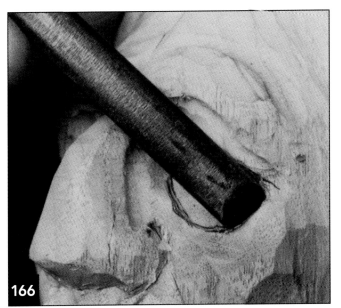

166

Finishing the cycle of this cut. I have formed a nice, large structure in which I can create all manner of really neat detail. Remember again, no amount of detail will look right if you don't have a good foundation for it to lay upon.

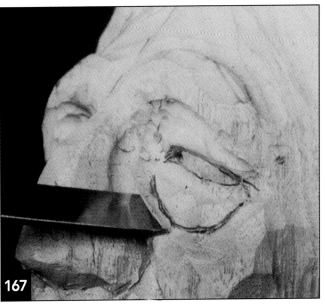

167

Now I am going to clean up these cuts with a nice, smooth transition of form, starting from the nose and continuing to the outer edge of the eye.

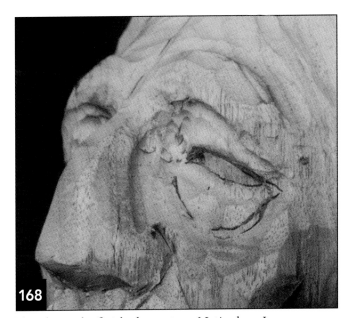

168

This shows the finished structure. Notice how I came smoothly off the nose and accented the upper part of the cheekbone as I came across with the cut.

169

This shows my having both sides pretty well developed up to this stage. Now I am going to quit here and work on the mouth and see if I can't develop this area a bit more. Notice that I have drawn the seven major muscles that form the lips. Also, I have indicated the two major chin muscles. Most of the time this area just appears as one mass, but oftentimes shows as a slight cleft in the chin.

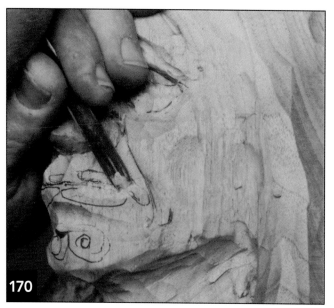

170

What I need to do now is separate and define all of these different muscles. The first one I define is on the outside of the actual opening of the lips. Not taking this into account is one of the major reasons we sometimes end up with a mouth that is far too narrow for the face.

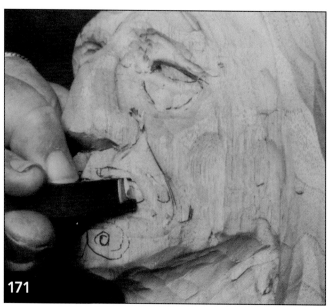

171

After I have isolated this muscle, I use a shallow gouge to round the lip structure down into the cut. This further develops the "dental curve."

172

Here is the completed series of cuts. Notice the prominent "shoveling" of the dental structure. This is a very prominent feature in many Native Americans.

173

I have now developed both corners of the mouth. For your visual reference, I am drawing a line that will represent the actual opening or parting of the lips. You can create all sorts of great expressions at this point by varying the shape of this line. Many times I use the general shape of a Cupid's bow exaggerated to various degrees. Pay special note to the spacing (one third down from the tip of the nose as a general rule).

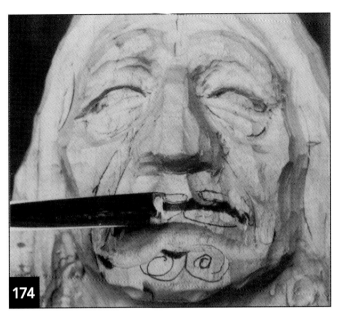

174

I am going to detail in the lips by first using a U-gouge to open up an area for the lips to lie in. This will follow the general shape we have previously drawn on.

175

A good view of the lips blocked out with the use of the U-gouge. Notice again the shape I have formed with this cut.

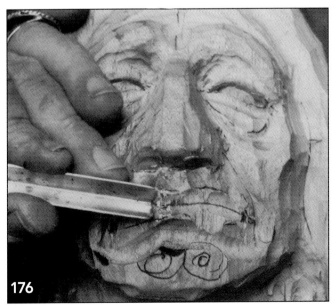

176

I have redrawn the line indicating the separation of the lips, and I am beginning to make this cut with a V-tool. The fuller the cut, the bigger the lips, and vice versa.

177

You can see how I have carried this clear to the corner of the structure. I normally cut my lips a little on the large side. (All the better to kiss with, Grandma.)

178

Now I have cut the entire length of the lips with the V-tool. Don't let the little chunk of wood that's missing bother you. We'll just develop whatever is left for us. I did glue a piece back on the upper lips. I, in infinite wisdom, had determined its loss would be intolerable.

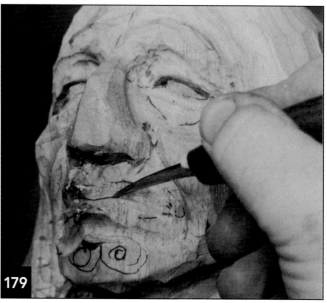

179

I now use a knife to sharpen or separate the lips. This cut is straight in.

180

I then cut a little wood from the lower lip to help round the lip a bit. I will also do the same to the upper lip. One must be cautious at this point not to create a large gap between the lips.

181

Here is a look at both lips fairly well formed. Notice the slight difference in the shape of each half.

182

Next I take a medium sweep gouge and finish rounding off the lower lip. This gets rid of most of the missing chips of wood I talked about earlier.

183

This next cut is one almost everyone forgets to do or doesn't know about. It is the separation of the "red" part of the lips away from the skin. I am doing this with a light cut using a deep U-gouge. All this cut does is create a very gentle transition of form that causes a shadow to form at this point, making the actual lip more visible. Without this separation of form, the whole lip area looks like one big pile of nothing.

184

This should make what I was trying to overstate very evident to the eye.

185

The next thing I am going to do is make a strong separation of the chin from the surrounding material. I am using a large U-gouge.

186

Here is the previous cut developed. Don't ever be afraid to move these cuts around a little and to use different gouges in executing the same. You have to force yourself to make aggressive cuts to develop a large, strong structure. You will constantly be amazing yourself with the wonderful things you can create using cuts you formerly thought would ruin a carving.

187

With a shallow gouge, I am rounding off the chin, keeping in mind that I want to make a smooth transition onto the form next to it.

188

This shows the chin fairly well rounded off. I used a #4, ¾" (18mm) gouge on this cut.

189

The next cut finds me making that smooth transition onto the jaw. I am still using the same gouge.

190

Here you can see the smooth transition from the chin to the jaw line. There is a little bit of minor cleanup and smoothing off to do yet, and we'll get that when we make one of the several go-arounds where we make the final clean up.

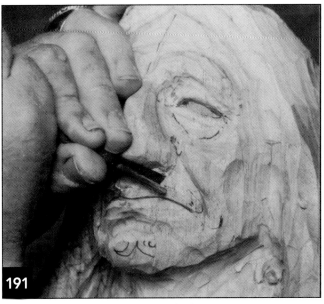

191

We need to detail the upper lip a little, so I am using a #11 gouge to create a small curl above the upper lip. This cut continues to roll down into the corner of the lips. You should be able to pick out this feature on some of the following photos.

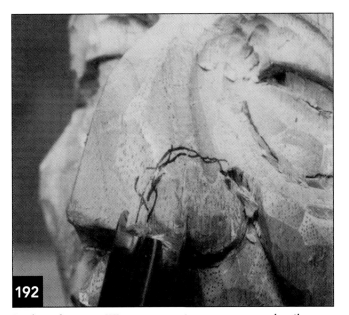

192

Back to the nose. We are now going to put some detail on this part of the face. We start by defining the nostril using a #11 gouge to separate it from the rest of the nose.

193

This gives you an idea of what this cut will produce. Notice there is still plenty of material on both parts so that a lot of carving can still be done if necessary.

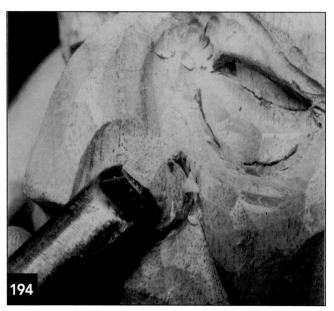

Next, I use a shallow gouge to shape the nostril.

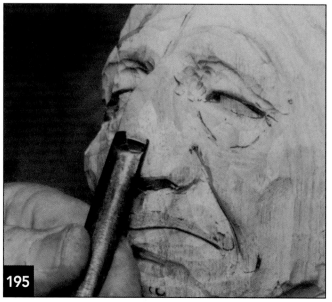

Here I am making that smooth transition along the side of the nose. Notice that I don't cut very far up the side of the nose. I need to save some wood about half way up to indicate a bit of swelling where the cartilage forms at the end of the nose bone itself.

You should be able to see the transition from the nostril to the nose in this photo.

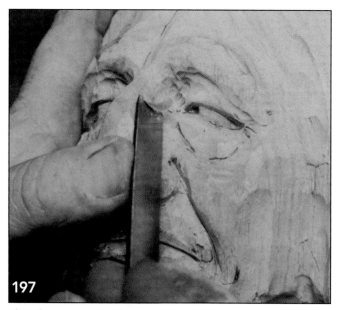

This shows my skipping over the middle of the nose so I can save or leave some wood, and cutting or smoothing out the cuts above it.

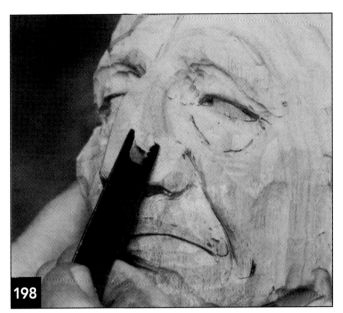

198

199

I need to drop back down to the end of the nose and round it off into a gentle ball.

This shows me finishing the rounding of the end of the nose. This will help define and increase the prominence of the "bump" or Native American nose that works so well in carvings of this sort.

– Requiem for a Dirt Road –

I often philosophize on life in general, and why things have happened to me as they have.

To fertilize my otherwise impotent mind, I often fantasize things and events that I feel would have greatly increased my stature in the world and environment I now live in. I never lived on a farm, so to speak, yet I often think of how it might have been if it were so. I do know it is darn hard work and as such, is something that does not endear itself to me with the relish of, say, hanging out with some friends smoking and drinking and just being a general ne'er-do-well. But I oftentimes think of it as such.

Requiem for a Dirt Road

Miles of dirt road behind me,
Life on the farm is hard but it's free.
A wife and a family, an old shade tree,
Milo, corn and beans, as far as you can see.

The blue skies of summer
Turns to fields of yellow grain.
The cold winds of winter,
Brought spring and her rain.
Like the circle of life
The seasons start again.
Happiness and joy.
Sorrow and pain.

　I spent my life
　Working on my daddy's farm.
　Working side by side in the fields.
　Then later on,
　I became my daddy's right arm
　So I traded in that mule for a wheel.

Now the dirt roads are gone
There's concrete and steel.
A new kind of farm,
A new kind of wheel.
But it doesn't change,
Things that are real,
And the love for the farm that I feel.

　Now my son spends his life
　Working on his daddy's farm.
　He worked by my side in the fields,
　Now he has become my strong right arm,
　So he traded for a new kind of wheel.

Miles of dirt roads behind me,
My life on the farm was hard but I was free.
My son and his family, now share this old shade tree
With milo, corn and beans,
　As far as
　　You can
　　　See.

CHAPTER 10

Detailing the Rest of the Carving

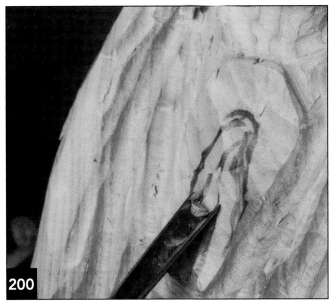

200

Let's let the face rest for a while and get on to some of the rest of the carving… starting with the decorative gorget in the front of his chest. I am going to start separating the two ties that are coming out of the center of it.

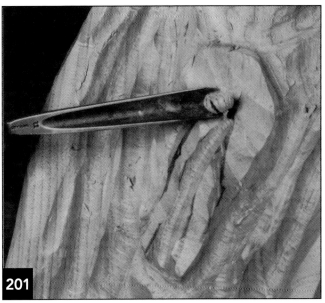

201

I have constantly visualized how I want these ties to disappear into the gorget. If you have trouble visualizing this, I suggest you make one up out of cardboard and string.

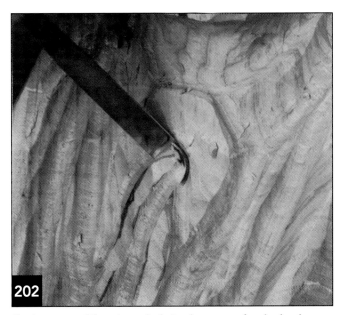

202

I'm just sort of forming a hole in the gorget for the leather ties to thread through.

203

Here I am rounding off the tops of the ties and rolling them down into the hole. It takes a lot of practice to be able to see what you're looking at and even more so to develop the eye-to-hand coordination to execute the cut.

204

With the ties fairly well defined, I am going to establish the outer boundary of the gorget itself. I am using a gouge that approximates the radius of the gorget. These are stop-cuts straight into the wood.

205

After outlining the gorget, I have come in from the side and cleaned up the cut.

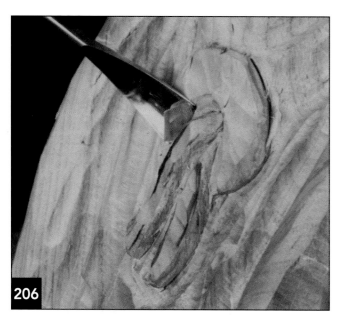

206

Now I'm doing the same thing with the leather ties, outlining them and cleaning the wood away from them.

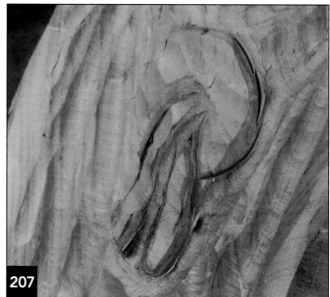

207

This shows the shell gorget finished except for some minor cleanup.

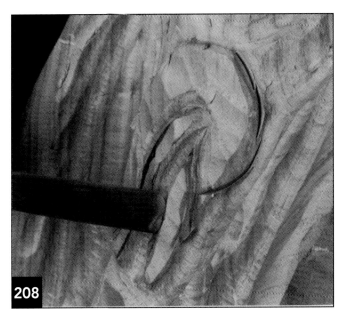

208

A little more defining on the ties where they lay on the chest area.

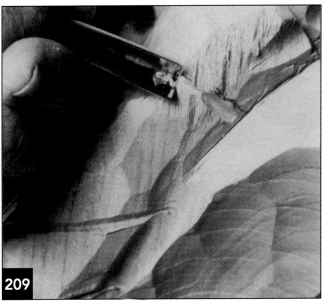

209

Now I am going to work on the textured wraps around the hair. Once the entire structure has been nicely rounded, I use a V-tool to separate or divide it into smaller parts.

210

Here is a frontal view of the developed hair wrap.

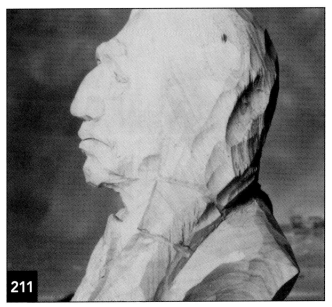

211

Now a side view. Notice how the entire structure we are working on is pretty much the same size throughout its entire length.

A good overall view of the entire piece. Notice I have already done one side, and I am demonstrating on the other. Keep the carving clean so we only have to carve it once.

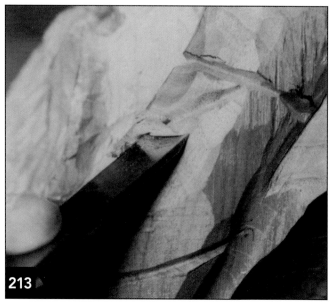

With the hair wraps fully separated with the V-tool, I will begin to further shape the various parts of them.

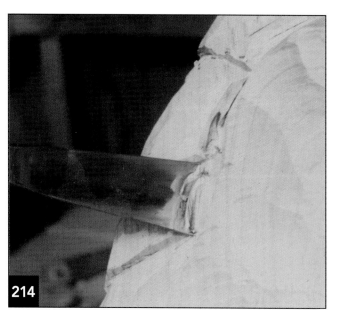

I am using a #5 or #6 gouge to shape the wraps. Be sure to carve clear around the structure in a manner of speaking, so that you can create a strong three-dimensional effect.

I continue this three-dimensional cut clear down to the end of the hair. These first cuts are stop cuts to be cleaned out next.

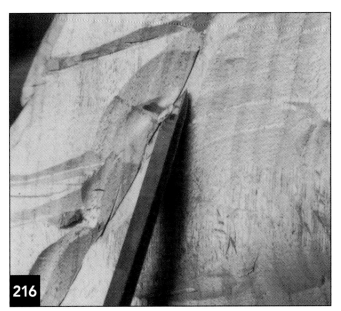

216

This shows me cutting in from the side to clean out the chips.

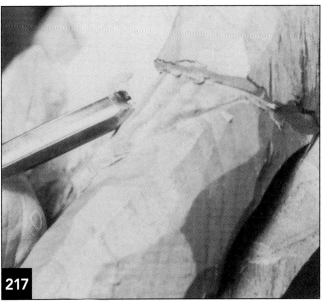

217

With this finished, I'll go ahead and texture the wraps I have created around the hair.

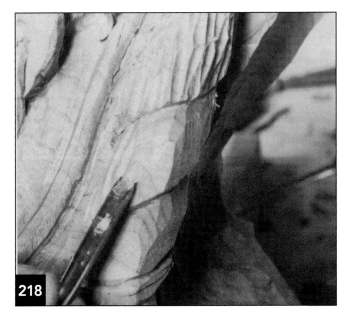

218

I am using a #11, ¼" (6mm) gouge to create this texture. I almost never use a V-tool to do this type of work, as it makes the area "too busy" and doesn't have any continuity with the rest of the carving in which we tried to use a softer approach.

219

Here I am finishing this area by carrying the texture on into the hair.

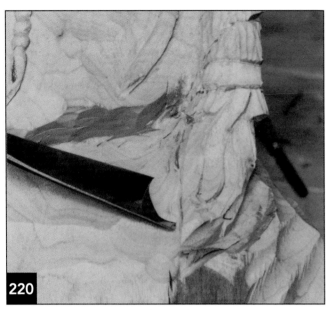

220

Since the hair, in this case, hangs down into the base area, I am going to undercut it so I have a positive separation.

221

This seemed to be going so good that I decided to cut completely around the hair.

222

Here I am doing the same thing on the other side.

223

With that done, I am using a large gouge to clean up the base in front.

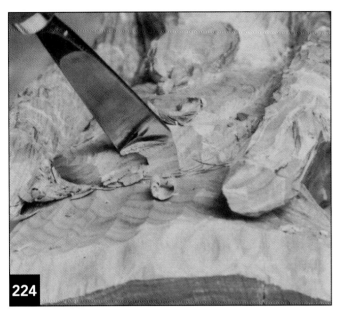

224

I am also undercutting where the actual bust ends and the base begins.

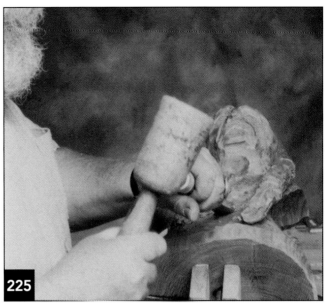

225

Here I have laid the carving back so I can clean up to these stop cuts.

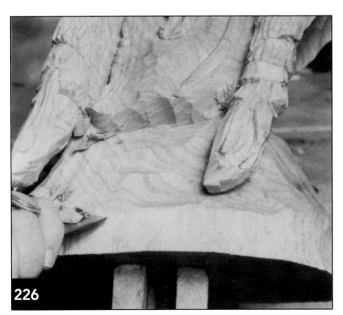

226

I am now finishing up the base. Notice in the corner of the picture how I have carried this shape on the base clear around the carving.

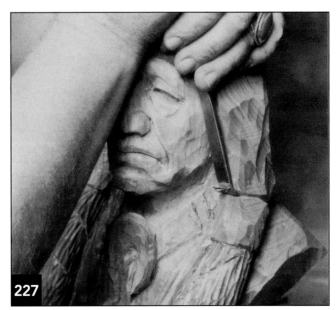

227

Back to the hair. If it seems like I am jumping around a lot, it is because you must constantly go around the carving, else you might develop too much of one area at a time. The entire carving must come together as a unit.

228

What do you think? Well, I'm tired of looking at his face. We should have been around the back side a long time ago, so let's spend a little time on the part that everybody hates to carve.

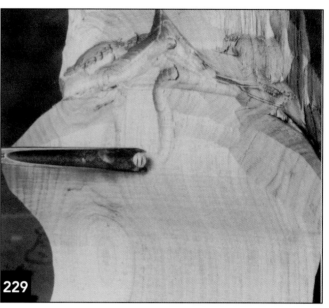

229

We really need to establish some sort of a neckline in the back, so I have rolled the hair in and down at the center. This creates an area for the neck to lay and gives me a chance to make some way of tying the hairpipe choker on so it doesn't fall off.

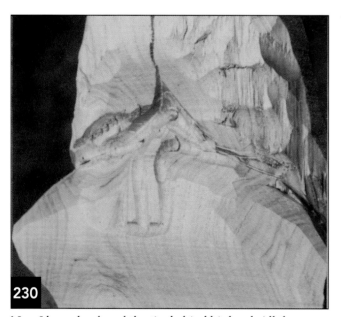

230

Now I have developed the ties behind his head. All they need is a little detail.

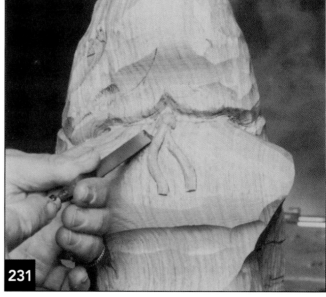

231

This shows the leather tie and the shoulder area in back just about finished. I'm not going to spend a lot of time fussing around here. You should be able to figure some things out for yourself.

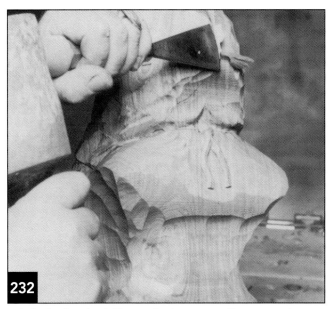

232

While I'm "out back" here, I had just as well get everything else taken care of, such as rounding off the hair and cleaning up any other loose ends and bad carving marks we have made.

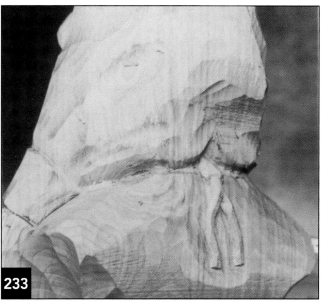

233

Except for a little hair, I think we are ready to move on to other parts. Too much time here and you start to feel like you're in the back seat of a taxicab.

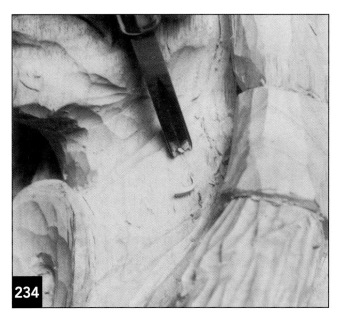

234

We are really starting to develop the detail now. Here I am detailing out the hairpipe necklace. If you don't know what these really look like, I would suggest you study one and see how it is put together. (I should talk. I just make mine up as I go along.)

235

Here I am using a U-gouge of suitable size to separate the bone hairpipes.

236

Once the different parts of the necklace are blocked in with a U-gouge, I can start rounding and developing the thing.

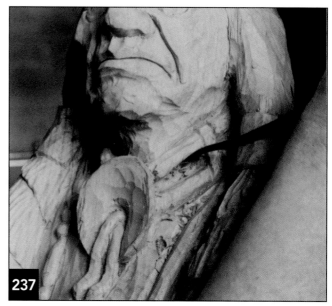

237

You have to really watch the grain of the wood at this point or else you'll find yourself making his neck bare.

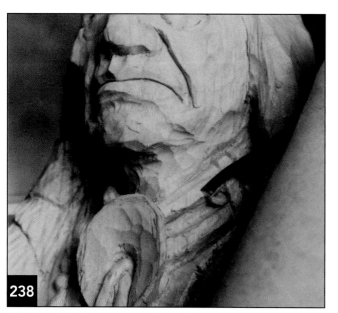

238

I finish up by cleaning out the inside areas and sharpening up the lines. I always save the hardest, most difficult, and most likely to screw up parts till last. Builds character.

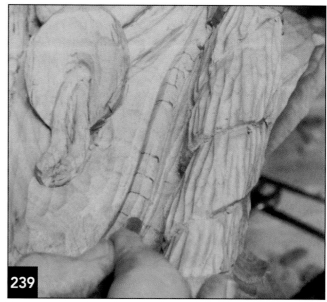

239

Here is another fun part. I am always amazed at the number of different ways some of my students tackle these areas. They almost always try to carve the detail first and end up with a hopeless mess. No discipline, I guess. Let's start at the beginning by marking off the areas that will be beads.

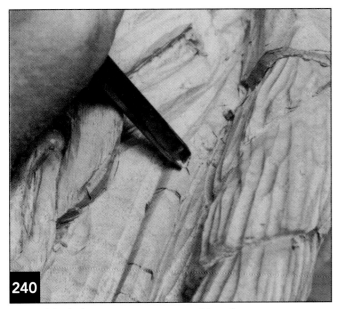

Now I block these areas out using a V-tool.

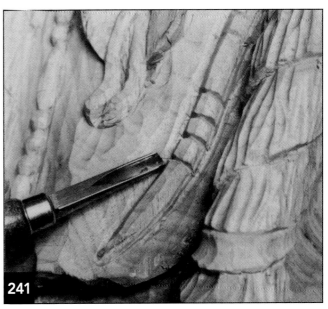

See what I mean? A real piece of cake.

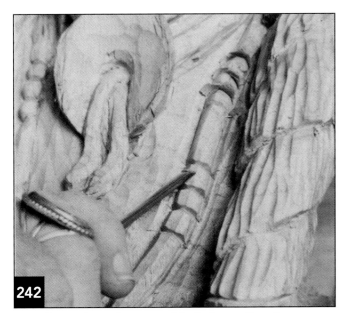

Now that we have these areas blocked out, all we have to do is shape them into round beads. Here I am using a small shallow gouge to do the job. Sometimes if you're lucky, you can find a tool with just the right shape to form these little guys.

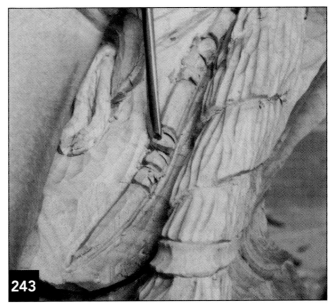

After cutting one side of the bead round, I come back from the other side and meet in the middle between beads.

244

Now I am cleaning up around the outer edge of the beads. Most people would stop here and consider this enough, but if you study close, you'll notice we only have a half-round bead sitting on top of the tunic. Let's put a real pro's touch on it. (Not mine. I learned this from another guy.)

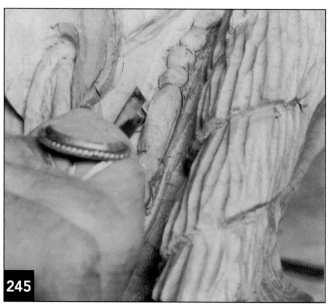

245

Here it is. Just nothing more than a little undercutting to make the eye "turn the corner and go around the bead."

246

Looking good, baby! Yours should be real close to this if you've paid any attention at all.

247

Now I want to give him a little age. I want to make a real strong point to you at this time. Wrinkles don't just happen. There is a definite pattern they follow, developed on the basic muscle structure that exists in all of us. Rule #1: This shows the general pattern of wrinkles as they MOST often occur, from the center of the eye and up. For more graphic proof, take a look at somebody with lots of lines in their face. Some of you need go no further than the mirror.

248

With that rule established, let's look at the next set of lines I have drawn. Rule #2: For the most part, wrinkles from the center of the eye and down tend to flow out, over and around the cheek. Now I'll admit it won't take too much looking to find somebody with lines strongly contradictory to what I have just told you. But you'll never get into trouble with these lines.

249

Around the mouth we see that the lines tend to follow the flow of the muscle structure we developed earlier in the book. Please understand that these are just some basic examples. Don't make the same lines over and over. Study people and get ideas and don't overdo it like he has a bad case of winterkill. A little can go a long way.

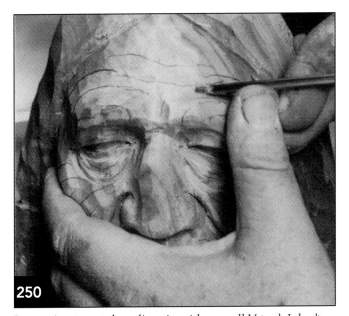

250

I am going to cut these lines in with a small V-tool. I don't try to follow the lines exactly, but rather use them as a general guide. I do try to keep a nice even flow going with no straight or jerky lines. Think "S" curves.

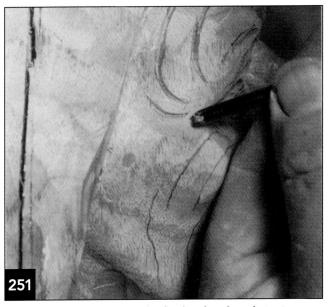

251

I have cut enough lines in the forehead and am bringing a few out from the corner of the eye. Lines like this help lead the eye from one part of the carving to another.

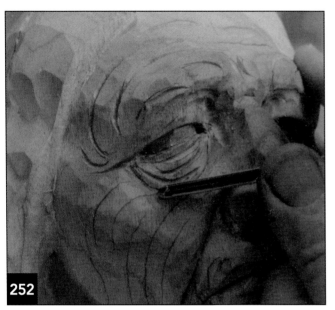

252

I like playing with different patterns in the mound of flesh I have created below the eye. Go easy here.

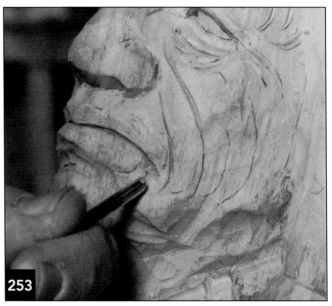

253

A few lines down the side of the face and some lines around the mouth and we should be pretty well set.

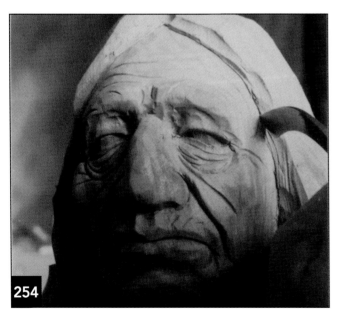

254

I am now going to make a hard line separating the hair from around the face. This is one of the few places I will use this type of line. Remember when you do this cut, follow the "S" curve of the face we so carefully developed earlier.

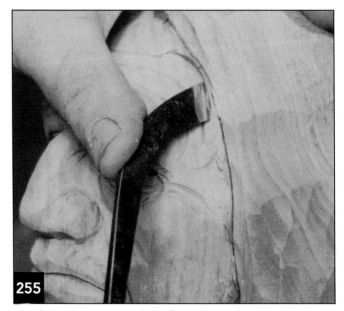

255

Finishing the cut around the face. The tool I am using is one of those oddball Cogelow clubs. It's called a bent skew, and if you can learn how to operate it, you'll wonder where it's been all of your life.

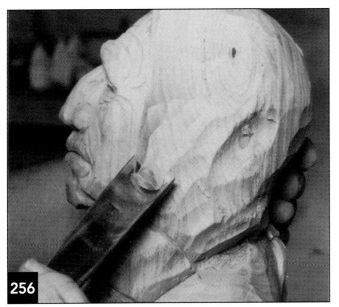

256

I am going to cut in some hair now by using a series of larger U-gouges. After so much work developing this nice soft approach to the sculpture, it just seems a shame to upset the serenity of the work with a pile of busy hair lines running all over the place. Again, this is my thought on this matter. By all means, everyone should screw up a few carvings by doing otherwise just for his own satisfaction.

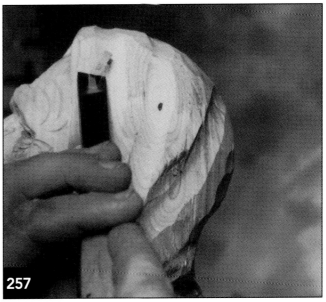

257

This shows how I soften the edges of the V-tool cuts, with a flat or very shallow gouge.

258

A little more work on the hair at the end of the wraps. Notice how I developed a little bit of the cloth tie hanging down onto the hair.

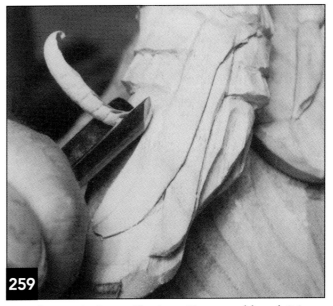

259

More hair again. I am still using a U-gouge, although it is somewhat smaller than the one I used on the upper hair.

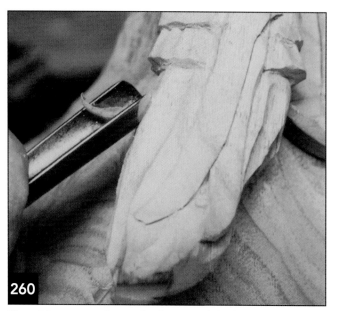

260

Since I have carved completely around the hair at this point, I also have to detail it out all the way around.

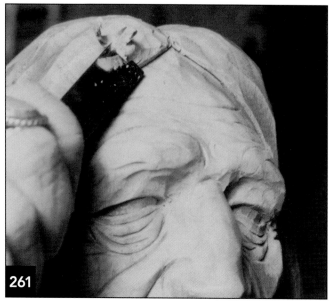

261

A little more rounding off of the hair on his head and I should be pretty well done. I always make about three cleanup passes around a carving when I am close to the end. This usually assures me of not missing any areas that will show up later on.

262

I need to finish the nose by cutting in a shadow for the nostril and defining the outside edge of the nostril. A small, medium-sweep gouge is used to cut a shallow opening in the bottom of this structure.

263

A similar tool is used to clean out this chip.

264

A gouge that approximates the curve of the nose is used to create a stop cut all the way up to the top of the nostril. This cut slices off any ragged wood fibers that are left. Be careful and undercut only so very slightly.

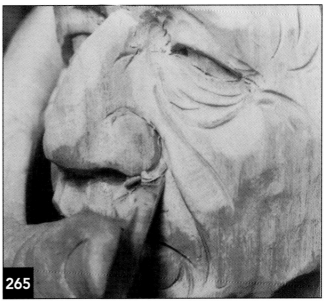

265

Again a suitable gouge is used to clean out this area. Do this cut only once. Succeeding cuts will only cause more fuzzies to form.

266

There. The finished nose. Nice and clean.

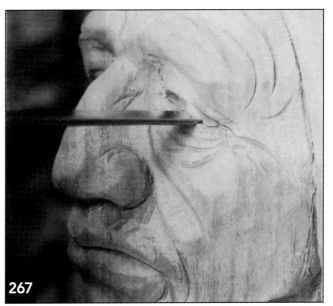

267

At this point, I will now bring the carving to life by cutting in the eyes. I almost always use a negative cut on the eye where everything within the pupil is removed.

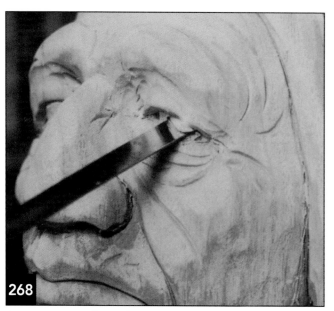

268

A #6 gouge usually works pretty good in here, but you need to experiment a little to find something that works good for you. I am cutting in and up under the upper eyelid.

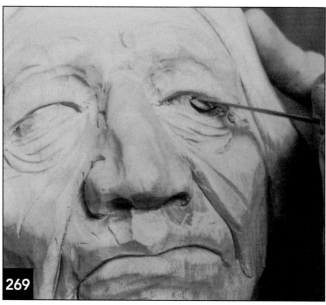

269

With that cut complete, I use a knife to cut straight in under the upper eyelid to remove the chip. You must create a hard shadow on this cut or it won't look right.

270

Now you can see the effect created by the negative eye. I will stain this area dark later on for an even stronger effect.

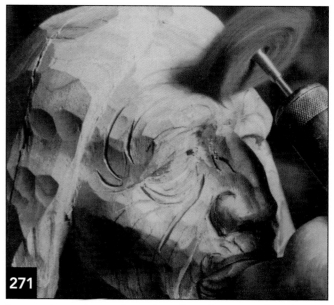

271

I guess the purist can have their fit at this time when they see the power tools used here, but I am not really doing any sanding, only using the scuff pads to soften some of the hard edges. This helps get rid of some of the fuzzies, but will not cover up any lazy or bad carving.

272

Go easy around the mouth or you will soften too much detail away.

273

I especially use the pads to soften the V-tool cuts used in creating the wrinkle lines.

274

When the pads wear down to a smaller size, I then get into some of the tighter spots.

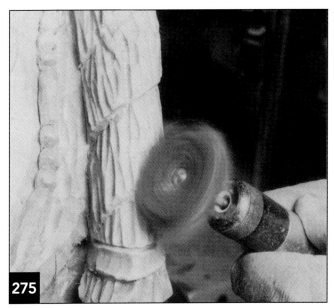

275

I pretty much touch base on the entire carving. What the heck, there is nothing wrong with using a little progress. If Michelangelo would have had jackhammers, you can bet he sure would have used them.

276

We're just about ready for the staining, but a last visual examination made me decide to add an upper eyelid to the eye. A very sharp V-tool will do this in fine fashion.

277

Using a V-tool to cut the upper eyelid.

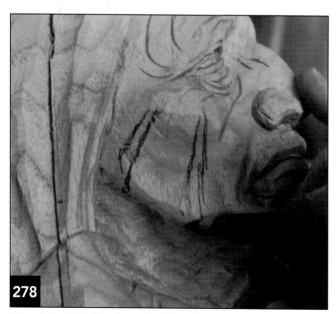

278

Now I decided that the side of the face needs a little punch, so I have drawn on the location of two muscle structures that sometimes exert themselves on strong, older faces. Remember, I am showing you this as I see it, not as it might be seen by another artist.

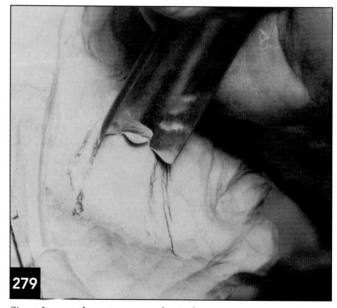

279

Since I want these two muscles to become more prominent, I am going to carve away some wood around them.

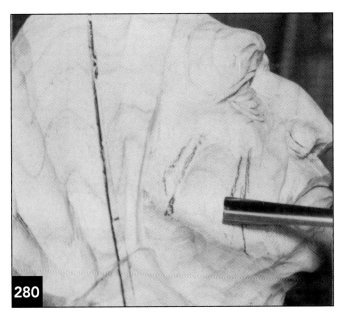

280

After removing some wood from between these two muscles, I am blending them in with that smooth transition of form.

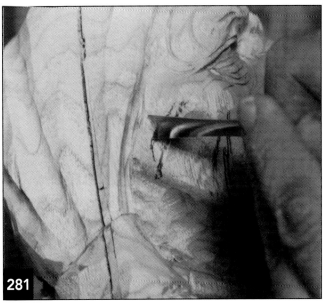

281

To emphasize them even more, I am going to take out some wood on the other side of them. You could work these muscles into an endless variety of patterns. One needs only to look at life for your ideas.

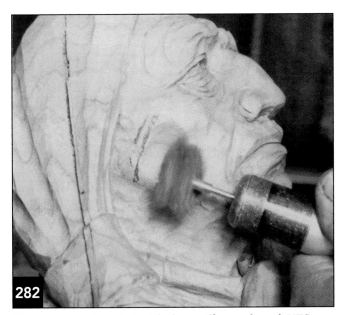

282

Okay, now one last shot with the scuffing pads and, YES, I am going to fill in that crack that opened up.

283

Ready to go as far as I am concerned. There is no sense in cluttering up the carving with a bunch of geehaws and fofraws. That's for egotists who like to show off. I feel that when the carving says what you want it to, stop.

284

I thought I would get my robust image in the act, too. Now you can see about how large this carving is.

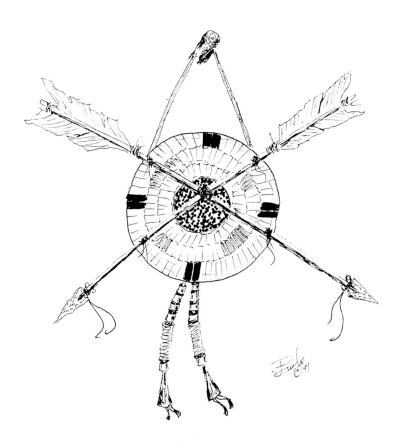

CHAPTER 11
Staining, Sealing, and Waxing

With the actual carving of the project completed, we have to put some type of finish on the wood. What I am going to show you here is the method I use most of the time.

Of course, you have to realize that different circumstances will arise that dictate using a finish other than what I will describe here.

285

286

I mix my own stains using oil paints and a turpentine substitute for a carrier. This shows my mixing a rich brown by graying some cad red light with a light green. I then richen the mixture with some cad orange. Believe me, there is no formula for these mixtures. You just have to go out and start doing it and see what happens. I will guarantee that the color you end up with will not be like anything you could squeeze out of a tube, and chances are you'll never be able to duplicate it.

Here I have taken a small amount of the mixed paints and added it to some of the solvent we are using. Start light as the color will darken as we go along.

287

288

I am brushing this "primary" color over the entire carving. I call this the primary color because all of the darks we develop later for accent will start with this color.

Now that I have covered the entire carving with our primary color, I am using a paper towel to soak up the excess stain. This is only to speed up the process. One really nice thing about this staining process is that in order to make the carving darker, you have to add more pigment to the stain mixture.

289

Adding burnt umber to some of the original color on the pallet, I accent certain areas with a darker color. Usually the hair and some of the trappings get this treatment.

290

Sculpture relies 100% on light to bring out the three-dimensional effect. Most galleries use proper light to increase the dramatic effect of the shadows. Trouble is, most people, upon buying a sculpture, take it home and set it wherever, without benefit of a good light and wonder why it doesn't look like it did in the gallery. To overcome this, I carefully dry-brush in all of the important shadows, so that no matter what the lighting, the carving is displayed with suitable emphasis to create a pleasing appearance. This photo shows my added shadows around the eye. A little study and practice will show you what works best.

291

Here is the carving stained and accented with color and shadows. Study this close for ideas.

292

The next step is to thoroughly seal the carving with a lacquer such as Deft or Krylon Matte. Don't use any "gloss" products or the finished piece will look like a ceramic. This picture shows me using a crumpled up brown paper bag to rub down the sealed carving. This removes any raised grain and rough spots without eating through the finish. This will leave the carving ready to be waxed.

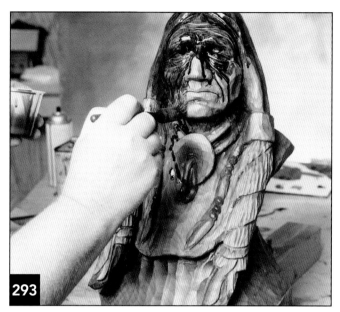

293

The first time you do this, you really suck wind. I'm using Watco Liquid Satin Wax "Dark." I first liberally brush it over the entire carving, making sure to get it into all of the nooks and crannies.

294

Right away, before the stuff dries, I wipe it off with a clean rag. I then use a brush to reach into the deep areas and pull the excess out onto the carving. This I also wipe up at some point. Of course, you have to quit sometime. It's a matter of personal judgment.

295

When the wax dries, I use a brush with long "natural" bristles to buff it down. After it dries overnight, I buff it down again. If I feel it needs more wax, I use Watco Satin Wax "Natural" on successive coats. Experimentation will teach what is best for you. I am comparing it here with our original clay sculpture. Not exact, of course, but close enough to have captured the essence.

296

One last look at the carving and yours truly and I'll leave you with a few parting words of thought. Always work to the utmost of your ability, for there is merit in every well-executed work of art, no matter what level you currently work at. Say what you want to say, not what others want to hear. Create no more than what is necessary to make your statement. Remember that "the mediocrity of the difficult, in no way compares to the excellence of simplicity." 'Nough said.

Basic Patterns

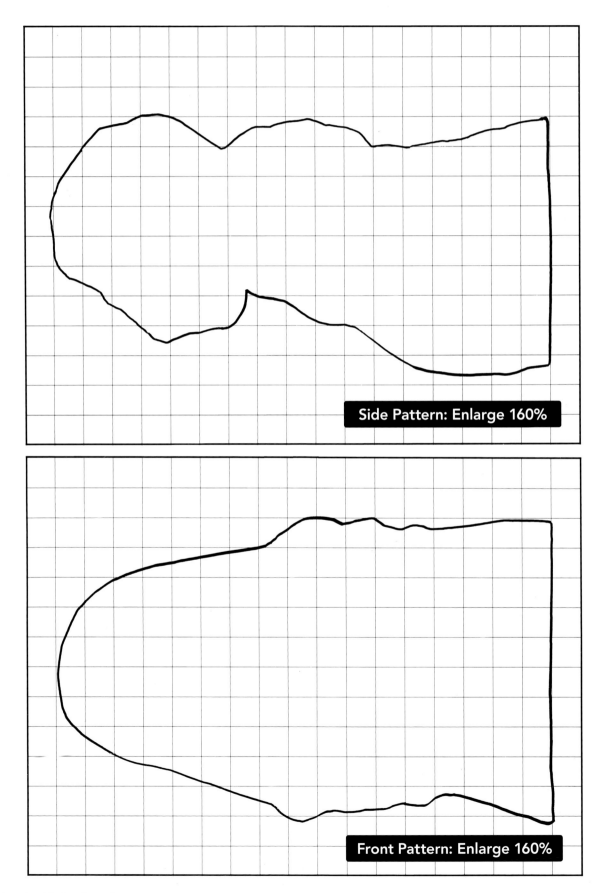

Side Pattern: Enlarge 160%

Front Pattern: Enlarge 160%

Index

More Great Books from Fox Chapel Publishing

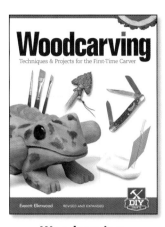

Woodcarving, Revised and Expanded
ISBN 978-1-56523-800-8 **$14.99**

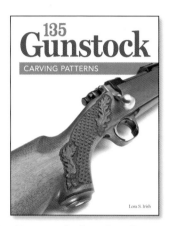

135 Gunstock Carving Patterns
ISBN 978-1-56523-795-7 **$16.99**

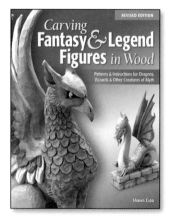

Carving Fantasy & Legend Figures in Wood, Revised Edition
ISBN 978-1-56523-807-7 **$19.99**

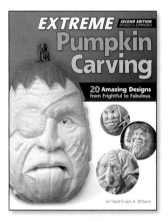

Extreme Pumpkin Carving, 2nd Edition Revised & Expanded
ISBN 978-1-56523-806-0 **$14.99**

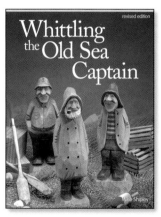

Whittling the Old Sea Captain, Revised Edition
ISBN 978-1-56523-815-2 **$12.99**

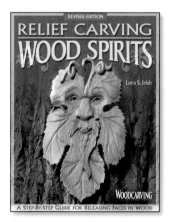

Relief Carving Wood Spirits, Revised Edition
ISBN 978-1-56523-802-2 **$19.99**

WOODCARVING
ILLUSTRATED

In addition to being a leading source of woodworking books and DVDs, Fox Chapel also publishes *Woodcarving Illustrated*. Released quarterly, it delivers premium projects, expert tips and techniques from today's finest carvers, and in-depth information about the latest tools, equipment, and materials.

Subscribe Today!
Woodcarving Illustrated: **888-506-6630**
www.FoxChapelPublishing.com